Medfield's Dwight - Derby House

Published by The History Press
Charleston, SC 29403
www.historypress.net

First published 2009

Manufactured in the United States

ISBN 978.1.59629.785.2

Library of Congress CIP data applied for.

Notice: The information in this book is true and complete to the best of our knowledge. It is offered without guarantee on the part of the author or The History Press. The author and The History Press disclaim all liability in connection with the use of this book.

Medfield's Dwight-Derby House

A Story of Love & Persistence

WRITTEN *by*
ELECTA KANE TRITSCH

THE History PRESS

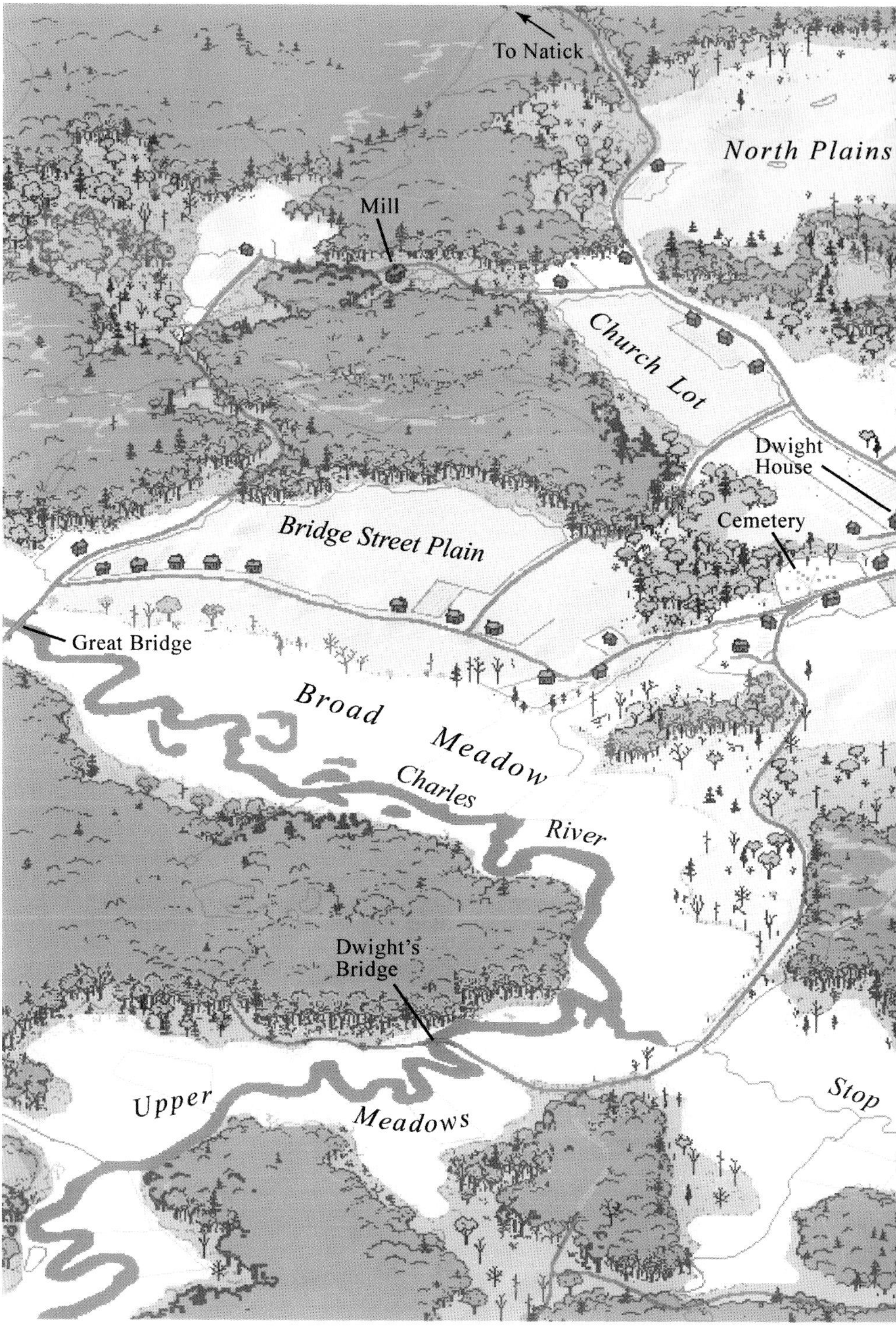
To Natick
North Plains
Mill
Church Lot
Dwight House
Cemetery
Bridge Street Plain
Great Bridge
Broad Meadow
Charles River
Dwight's Bridge
Upper Meadows
Stop

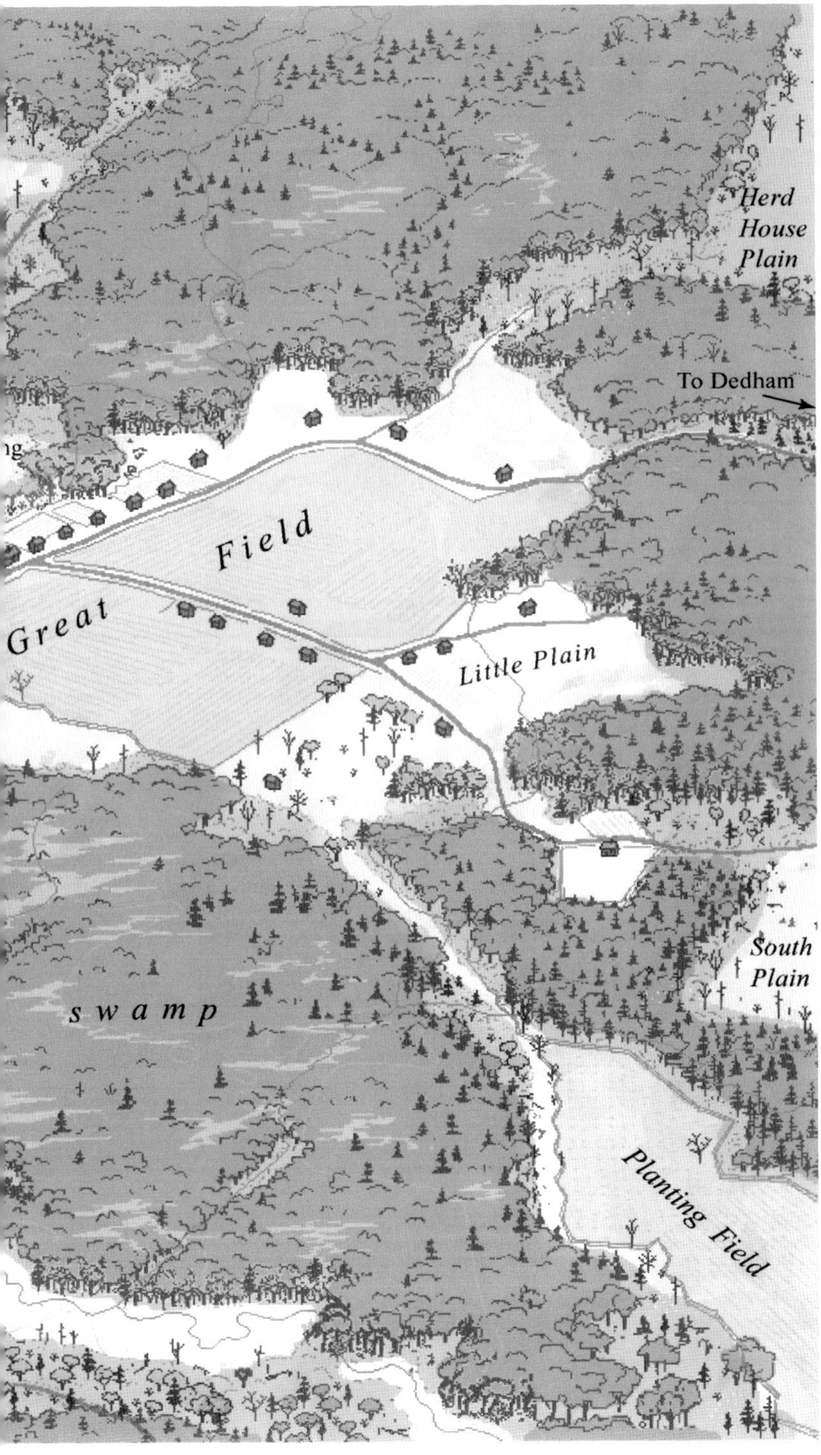

Medfield,
circa 1670.
Conjectural reconstruction by Vin Antill.

Contents

Acknowledgements and Notes

A fourteen-year project involves the labor and knowledge of more people than can ever be properly recognized. A few were special contributors from the start: Victor Peskett, East Anglian researcher extraordinaire, who found the Dwights in obscure parish records; Bob Hanson, Dedham historian, ever gently steering me in the right direction; Richard DeSorgher, activist and ultimate source of Medfield history; Jackie Wile, who encouraged and dug with me; Vin Antill, who worked for ten years to map seventeenth-century Medfield; and Mike Standley, the gray wizard whose wisdom and grace made the whole preservation project work.

I am grateful for the fellowship of the Medfield Archeology Advisory Committee; the instant preservation education provided by Mary Turkel, Bob Majors, Larry Sorli and their crews; the cooperation and patience of research staff at the Medfield and Dedham Historical Societies, the Massachusetts Historical Society, the Peabody Essex Museum Phillips Library and, especially, Susan Lintelmann and Debby McKeon-Pogue of the United States Military Academy Archives.

Funding for parts of this research came from the Massachusetts Foundation for the Humanities and the Friends of the Dwight-Derby House. Special thanks are due to Friends' chairman John Thompson and to the responsive and able assistance of House Manager Cheryl O'Malley.

A whole separate chapter of thanks is due to writing group friends who read and reread; to my husband Geoff, who always believed; and to Saunders

Robinson, senior commissioning editor at The History Press, who saw the story behind the façade.

A note on images: Unless otherwise credited, photos are by the author. Line drawings of conjectural Dwight-Derby House construction phases are by Lawrence A. Sorli.

A note on sources: Sources directly referred to in this book are given full citation in the endnotes. Readers interested in additional reference material should go to the book's website, www.loveandpersistence.com. The quotations used are often drawn from much longer documents, most of which have been transcribed and are available to researchers. See the website for list and details.

Aha!s

If we knew what we were doing, it wouldn't be called Research.
—A. Einstein

I am a historian. I'd love to say that I'm a detective, an explorer, a storyteller, a theoretician, but basically, I poke around in old documents and decrepit cardboard boxes, clamber through cobwebbed buildings and cat briar trying to find something that doesn't exist anymore: the past. At least eight, possibly nine, times out of ten, I start with little notion of what I'm looking for and certainly no idea of what I'll find. At the other end of the search, the product is almost invariably a surprise, usually a satisfying one, but between start and finish there is a lot of slow and admittedly uninspired research.

There are reasons I keep at this, however. I call them the Aha! moments. I have discovered that lots of people now call serendipities Aha! moments. Google, the new-age encyclopedia, has pages of citations for these epiphanies, including recent neurological research into their phenomenology, and I have learned that Oprah Winfrey dedicates an entire feature in her magazine to them. The American Heritage College Dictionary (1993) offers a classic definition: "aha—interj. Used to express surprise or pleasure." Of course, the venerable Oxford English Dictionary (the compact 1971 edition) offers by far the most interesting analysis:

> ***Aha***...[a combination of the two interjections Ah! and Ha! formerly written separately a ha]...*An exclamation expressing, with*

different intonations, surprise (arch. or obs.), triumph or satisfaction, and mockery or irony.

In my world, the interjection comes up when, along the way between the start and end of a project, I stumble across small discoveries that bring coherence to disparate facts. Sometimes they are missing links. Sometimes they provide context that transforms a mundane act into a life-changing decision. I have waded through projects with only one Aha! moment, finding at the end that I had to struggle to fashion more than an FYI report with the results. Once in a long while, though, a project comes along so filled with Aha! moments that it beats out fiction for a good read.

The house on Frairy Street was such a project. I only set out to sketch a quick timeline of who did what when to this house threatened by development—something to grab attention, to rally support for an effort to save the building on its quaint village lot from morphing into condos.

Aha!s started coming before the research even began. The poking and clambering that followed slowly exposed whole families of men and women who lived at, built and died at the house on Frairy Street. Remarkably, through it all, the Aha!s never stopped, each contributing its small asterisk of significance to elevate the story from a local tale to a four-hundred-year portrait of American life in a New England town.

I never had a house speak to me as loudly as this one did, nor families long dead clamor so clearly to be heard. I am left with an insistent, nagging sense of responsibility that it's up to me to tell the story.

Pink Elephant

Medfield didn't know what it had at first, of course. It was a decaying hulk of a house smack in the middle of everything—a faded pink elephant facing on Meetinghouse Pond. Someone had taken stabs at fixing it up over the years. Two dormers were vinyl-sided yellow. The front of the house and one side had been spray painted with what was meant to be old red but turned out tired pink. Most of the white trim was still peeling, and the clapboards on the ell were still a dirty yellow. The center chimney had lost some top bricks. The gutter across the wide façade was broken. And the black front door, held together by rusting L-irons, was shrouded with overgrown shrubs around its granite doorstep.

Out back was a breezeway to a small carriage barn. Both were a mess—screens torn and vines growing through the breezeway; holes in the barn roof and under its walls where a skunk or woodchuck—something good-sized, anyway—had made its way in.

Mostly what had the town worried was that the property would get bought by some developer who would build brick-box condos all over the half-acre lot. That would complete the ruination of Frairy Street's east end, permanently alter that quaint New England feel the town was so proud of. Frairy Street had already taken quite a blow. A decade earlier, the sprawling, shingled Queen Anne that had defined its corner for a century had been carefully ignored by its absentee owner until an engineer could declare it unsafe for habitation. Then it was razed. "The Colonial Building" went in there—built right into the cellar of the old house and rising three stories

SAVE THIS HOUSE! September 1995. *J. Wile photo.*

high, a flat-faced behemoth bigger even than the old meetinghouse across the street. Colonial, indeed.

Few things, they say, are so bad that nothing good comes of them. In the case of the Colonial Building, indignation at the eyesore mobilized the citizenry, or a vocal part of it, to the cause of historic preservation. So when the decrepit place next door finally sprouted a For Sale sign in 1995, a lot of people began agitating to save the old Derby house before it was too late. There was a committee, a resolution at town meeting, a pitch to actually buy the house for the town.

Come Medfield Day in September, as small town businesses and volunteer groups touted their wares from booths around Meetinghouse Pond, the pink elephant that faced them was draped with a hand-lettered white-sheet banner:

SAVE THIS HOUSE

Somebody had talked the owner into letting people inside the house. A lot of them were charmed by its quaintness. A lot more were appalled by its condition. A few got very excited about what they found. One of the first-floor front rooms had an uncased ceiling beam—chamfered, the excited ones said, with lamb's tongue stops—and the room had a raised sill. The bake oven in the huge kitchen fireplace was built into its rear wall. Both were clear signs, to an eye that knew First Period from Georgian architecture, that the house's outside wasn't telling the whole story. This was not a comfortably late colonial building. Pieces, at least, of the old Derby house dated back to the seventeenth century.

CHAPTER I
Dwights
1609–1790

In the Beginning

The story of the first Dwight on Frairy Street begins with hints and conjectures among the tightly scrawled parish registers of the Ipswich archdeaconry in England.[1] Timothy was the youngest of William Dwight's three sons, born about 1609 in the village of Woolverstone, near the East Anglian coast. Nearby was Ipswich, the market town that drew business and fleece from this sheep-farming region. Ipswich was also the heart of Puritan country.

There is no hint that the Dwight brothers had sisters at home—but then, the records of their births, like Timothy's own, may have been lost. The Dwight relatives who lived in surrounding towns appear as middling farmers, better off than common laborers, owning some fields "copyhold" but supplementing these by working for larger landowners as well.[2]

In 1629, when Timothy was twenty, his father and mother died in quick succession and were buried just a week apart. Timothy would have derived little from the estate. Traditional inheritance patterns would assign all, or at least a double portion, of any landholdings to Nicholas, the eldest, while brothers John and Timothy might divide the rest. John, the second son, may have come into some money or some acreage earlier, when he married. Timothy was still single, though. He probably lived with one of his brothers and worked their land.

THE DWIGHT FAM

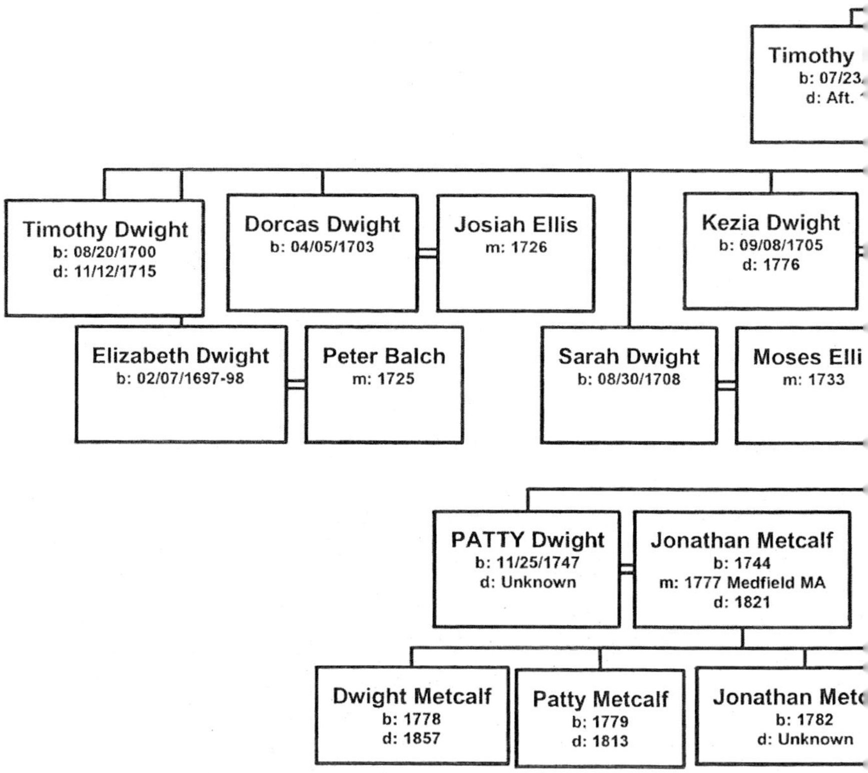

Not a complete family tree. Capitalized names are those who owned the Dwight-Derby House.

FRAIRY STREET

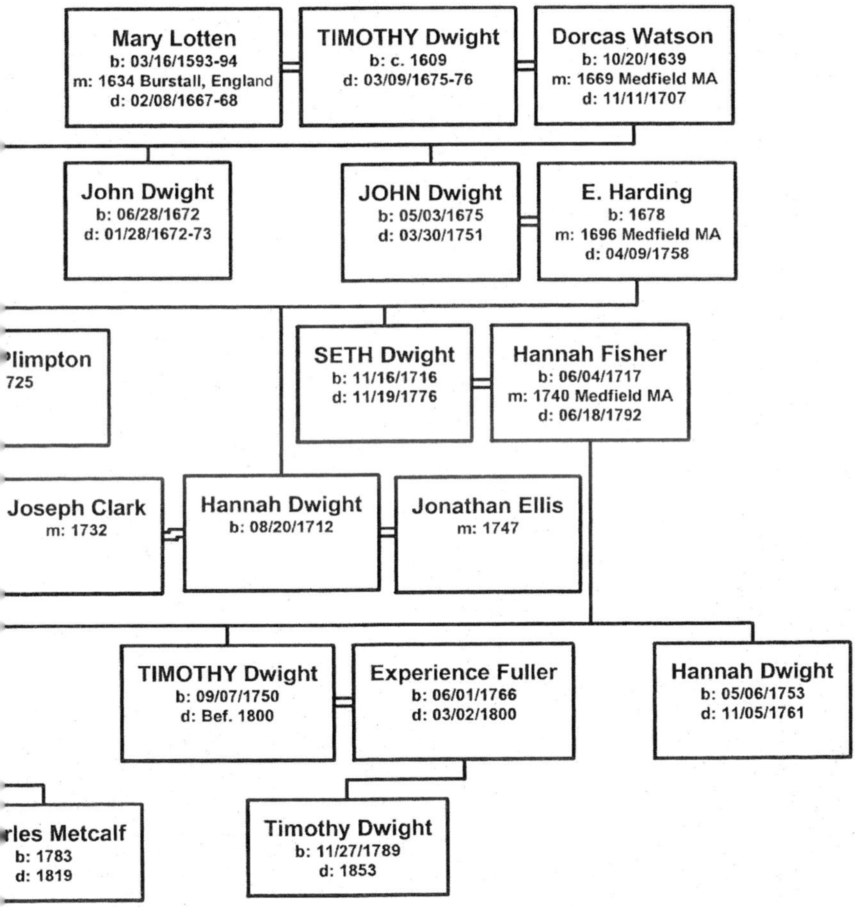

The prospects for Timothy's future were not good in seventeenth-century East Anglia. The region was in the throes of a major economic depression caused by reduced demand for wool, its single staple farm commodity. This affected both farm employment and work in the processing and mercantile trades, further limiting Timothy's options for improving his standing. Then, too, there was a spiritual call to the New World heard by many of the region's devout. Towns such as Ipswich and Dedham became known as hotbeds of Puritan unrest, inflamed by the reforming thought and inspired preaching of such clerics as Timothy Dalton, the Puritan minister of Woolverstone between 1615 and 1636.

Five years passed. John and his wife Hannah began a family in Woolverstone. Their first child was named Hannah for her mother. The second, a son, was named Timothy (perhaps for a family member or their minister, Timothy Dalton). John Dwight's own namesake John was born two years later. Then the John Dwights left East Anglia behind. When sailing season began in 1635, they set out for the New World—possibly as part of a group that sailed with the Reverend John Rodgers—despite Hannah's advanced pregnancy. Daughter Mary was born at sea on July 25. A year later, John Dwight became a founding member of the new community of Dedham, located southwest of Boston in the Massachusetts Bay Colony.[3]

Letters came and went between Old and New Worlds, as did stories, as ships' captains and visitors returned to home ports and home parishes, reporting on the welfare of the little congregations that braved the wilderness in the name of God and a better life. Timothy Dwight, at home in Woolverstone, heard the call, for his brother John's tale was clear evidence of the wonder-working providence of God. Right from the start, Timothy heard that John was one of the highest ranked men in this new town of Dedham.

The process of ranking "persons and estates," as it was called, was an essential part of organizing a New England town. It included consideration of traditional factors, such as inherited social position. It also weighed a man's civic worth to the community. A minister, say, was essential to the spiritual welfare of a new town; an educated man or soldier, able to lead in government or war, was awarded extra weight. Finally, in recognition of the benefits of stability, a significant factor in ranking was a man's marital status and family size. When all the weighing was done, a rank-ordered list was drawn up of every man in the community, and that list served as the basis for apportioning land grants to first settlers and newcomers alike.

John Dwight's high rank on the Dedham list could not have been predicted from his situation back home. Certainly, John had taken some money with him when he sailed, but more than gold counted in this raw new society. From the beginning, John Dwight had made his commitment to Dedham clear. He had come with a family, a religious conviction and a leadership ability that put him into office right away as one of Dedham's governing selectmen. For that commitment, John received his reward in land: twelve acres to start, the largest possible allotment for house lot and home fields. Over the next twenty-five years, that allotment would grow to a sizable country estate, and his children would inherit more than their grandfather back in England could ever have imagined.

Timothy, though, must have done a lot of imagining as he worked on Nicholas's land. The voice from the New World must have been clear.

> *Come over, little brother. Come share the profits of a new land while you're still young enough to use 'em. But better to marry afore ye come, for there are few enough females in New England worth the looking. More, as well: you'll begin with twice the land here if you're wed, than you would a single man. And every grant depends from that first allotment. Remember what I say. Estate begets estate.*

Three towns away from Nicholas and Timothy's home in Woolverstone lay Burstall. There Timothy, age twenty-five, found Mary Lotten (or did they meet at Ipswich market, or in the Dedham church?). Mary was forty years old, next to youngest of a family of ten. Perhaps she was not much of a looker, but Timothy must have had more on his mind than appearance when he set out to find a wife. Mary was the Lotten girl who had stayed home to tend her widowed mother while twenty years of her adult life ticked away. A woman with that sense of duty, of persistence and patience, would be a good helpmeet with whom to face the unknown. And the urgency was the same. Mary, like Timothy, had come into her own, whatever there might be of it. Her mother had died two years earlier, and she wondered what in heaven's name to do with herself for the rest of her life. When she looked at Timothy she saw a strong one. His head grazed the summer beam; his manner combined the respect proper in a younger man with a passion for what life had never offered. So she grabbed for the brass ring, and they were married after the harvest in 1634, just in time for the fall sailings to the New World. And who knows? Perhaps God in his goodness might yet see fit to bless them with children, even with her at such an advanced age.

The ship docked in Boston and eventually, Mary and Timothy found their way out the Country Road through Cambridge and Watertown, through the progressively wilder landscape of Roxbury to Dedham. There John Dwight took his younger brother under his wing.

August 1638 marks the first dated reference to Timothy in the Dedham records, when brother John was granted a half-acre of land in compensation for the half-acre he turned over to his brother "for situation of his house next the hither end of that ground which the wheelwright had."[4] The two brothers lived across East Street from each other, among a cluster of houses that looked out over a brook first called the Little River, later Dwight's Brook, and known as Wigwam Brook today. This would not be the last time Timothy Dwight would build beside a brook.

Altogether, Timothy Dwight's first land grant totaled six acres—a married, respectable, childless man's home lot. It came to him as his right when he signed his name to the Dedham Covenant, signifying his commitment to the new community and acceptance of its regulations. The signature also enfranchised him, and he appeared on record at his first town meeting in November 1638.

A lot of organizing went on in a new town. That same November, the Dedham church was also assembled. Its first members came together and each made a personal profession of faith to satisfy the others that they were in accord on matters of theology and belief. Just two months after the church was gathered, Hannah Dwight, John's wife, was received as a communicant. John hesitated, however, his conscience not yet comfortable with the particular tenets to which the other members subscribed.

Three months of soul-searching and, one has to think, well-intentioned persuasion on the part of his wife and others led him to reconsider. "[April 1639] John Dwite who after some scruples wherein ye Church waited a good while for satisfaction yet gave good, comfortable satisfaction to ye church"[5] and thus qualified as a founding father. Timothy watched. There were other things to watch as well. Timothy watched Hannah and John take their two youngest girls to be baptized into the faith, with two older children following behind. There were no babies in Timothy and Mary's house.

Timothy watched the selectmen grant dozens of acres of town land to its inhabitants. In 1640, two years after Timothy's arrival, the town voted to turn a tract of valuable plow land over to private use. He was granted two acres, one rood and fifty-seven rods of land. Brother John received eleven acres. During those first years in Dedham, Timothy was constantly playing catch-up with his older brother. There were a number of strikes against him, over which he had no control. He was—and always would be—two years behind John in land grants. He also did not have children. Timothy did what he could to prove his worth to the community. He took part in a survey team that defined the boundaries of Dedham's vast holdings, but that contribution to the communal good, although it raised his rank in the community, could not compare to his brother's position as selectman.

It appears that John and Timothy worked together, trying to even out the field. Timothy made sure he didn't repeat his brother's mistakes. "30th of ye 6 mo 1640 Timothy Dwite was received into ye church giving good testimony of ye frute of ye ordinances in his conversion to god."[6] No scruples of conscience there, despite the fact that his wife Mary never did become a communicant in Dedham.

By 1643, Timothy's efforts began to produce results: four more acres of land fit for plowing or mowing. That same year, he became one of seven selectmen elected to carry out the town's business. Probably not coincidentally, John was one of the others. In the following year, a distribution of woodland in town netted Timothy three acres: one-third of John's allotment, rather than the one-fifth Timothy had received during his first years.

The 1648 records show him appointed to assist the surveyor in laying out a three-hundred-acre land grant in the town. His own house was valued at fourteen pounds, twelve shillings. He still looked out his upper-story window at John's house, worth twice as much, but *only* twice as much. And tall, sharp-sighted Timothy became a member of the town militia, for which he was called "Corporal Dwight" in the 1650 records.

* * * * * * *

In 1650, an event occurred that affected Dedham—and Timothy—forever. He served on the committee assigned to evaluate the northwest corner of the Dedham Grant. Here, the governor's council wanted to establish a "praying Indian" village for the Natick tribe, under the auspices of the Reverend John Eliot and the Society for the Propagation of the Faith. Eliot had gone over the heads of Dedham authorities, proposing directly to the governor and council that a number of English-style settlements be established with government assistance, to introduce amenable tribes in the colony to the benefits of living in English ways. Eliot recommended village sites in the vicinity of established native camps where he had already made significant progress spreading the gospel and converting the inhabitants to Christianity.

His first Indian town had been a failure. Nonantum (Newton) was located too close to English settlement to be left alone. Crops were trampled and fences were knocked down (echoes of residential prejudice still heard in the present century).[7] Eliot's next proposed location for a model village was at a fall line on the Charles River where a band of Nipmuc Indians had long had a seasonal encampment.

The missionary's plan met with strong resistance at the local level, not because a handful of Englishmen might be displaced or because the Indians would be too close, but for more pragmatic reasons. The two-thousand-acre parcel in question included a very useful source of water power.[8] The parcel was also a significant block of common land that Dedham had expected to divide, at some time in the future, among its own townsmen. Two thousand acres taken away from Dedham were so many acres taken away from the inheritance a man could give his sons, or from the dowries of his daughters. The action went against the best interests of every English freeman in the Dedham grant, and they were not going to let their land go without protest. "For as much as…the motion about the Accomadation of the village to be erected for the Indians at Natick is a matter of great concernment in many respects, it is thought meete to nominate & depute…men…to take a carefull and special view of the Lands."[9]

The men deputed as a committee to check out the area might have canoed there, up the Charles River from Dedham's town landing, but they would have been hampered by a stretch of rapids and might well have had to portage around the sachem Noanet's fish weirs. More likely they went overland, walking one of the ancient trails that crisscrossed the region from one native camp to another. They headed out of the village and northward, through the Springfield Dividend to the bank of the Charles, then westward to the big Indian camp at the falls: the part of Dedham called the Natick Dividend. They were about to lose two thousand acres of this land because of political pressure that reached all the way up to the Crown.

In fact, Dedham was offered a choice of tracts to the west, beyond English settlement, as compensation for what it was losing. Eventually, the townspeople would settle for Pocumptuc, a wilderness tract of eight thousand acres that would make a few townsmen wealthy and be the death of others under the name of Deerfield. But during this first Natick survey, the men were thinking of what they would lose, not what some future generation might hope to gain.

The next day was getting on when they were ready to return, and the trail they'd come on was tricky footing in the dark. So they struck out south from Natick, following the river still as it took a great bend upstream toward its headwaters. After a few minutes on steep banks, they emerged on gentler ground that opened out to fresh meadow and patches of open swamp. This was rich land compared to Natick—easy land to put to use. They and the Indians had done so for years. They had harvested hay and reeds, withies and alder saplings for fodder and furnishings, baskets and wigwam poles. But mostly, the Dedham men saw the broad meadows as an endless God-given supply of hay. There weren't many things to be had without work in a new settlement. So this western edge of Dedham they named Medfield. "Meadfeilde," some of them wrote. It was one long stretch of meadow hay along the river's edge.

The men reached the ancient east–west Indian trail and turned toward home. This trail was wide enough to walk two abreast or ride. A tumbril heaped high with hay could bump its way back home through the flat, level terrain by the river, up a slow slope to a field cleared by natives in the old times, before the pox had spread across Massachusetts Bay and cleared the land of most of its heathens.[10] The Great Field, as the men called it, spread remarkably flat and fertile for a score of rods on the south side of a brook.

* * * * * * *

The sound of water burbling over rocks was clear from where the men sat at the crossroad. It wasn't much of a crossroad, really, just a trampled spot where the main east–west track met up with the north way. A footpath disappeared southward, barely visible in the overgrowth of the old planting field.

"Fair size brook up there?"

Timothy Dwight had never walked this way.

"Nah. Just a piddling thing." Joshua Fisher tipped up his felt hat brim to wipe the sweat away. "Flows into that swamp patch we crossed back a bit, by the river. We'll pass more of it up ahead, alongside the trail. Year-round, though, from what I've seen."

Fisher had seen as much as any Englishman in these parts. He was fifty years old and had been the unofficial town surveyor since Dedham was founded fourteen years ago.

"Sweet water," John Gay offered. Gay owned outlands in this direction and knew the resources.

One of the packhorses snorted and tossed its head. Dwight gathered himself up from where he'd stretched out long legs and laid a calming hand on the horse's neck.

"How long'd you say we've still to go till town?" he asked.

A brief frown of calculation as Fisher glanced at the sun. "Midday, maybe, were we ahorse. It'll be near dark afoot, though. Trail swings south up ahead, past the rocky woods, and that's a long way round the crow flies."

John Gay nodded agreement.

"Well then," Dwight said, "I'll just water the Boys here"—he reached for a second lead rope—"while the water's still in reach." He headed toward the brook as the animals docilely walked alongside, long accustomed to his direction.

"Hold up." Another long-legged man rose and moved to join him. John Dwight's graying hair proclaimed him the older brother.

Watering the Boys was simply done. The brook they had heard was only a few rods north of the crossroads, and the animals waded right in to drink at the fording place. Timothy and John could make out little of the brook's upper reaches, hidden in a tangle of bushes and briar, but below the ford it stumbled and tripped over a spill of boulders, finally curving out of sight two hundred yards ahead. Between the Dwights and the curve, gentle sloping upland lay on both sides.

"A likely spot, isn't it?" Timothy considered.

"More civilized, for sure, than much that we've surveyed these past days," John replied. The men were returning less than impressed by the lay of Natick's land.

"A man would do worse than build hereabouts, I'm thinking."

Timothy cast a sidelong glance at John as he gave a gentle tug on the animals' reins. There were a lot worse places to settle in Massachusetts Bay. A crossroads and a well-worn track; an old cleared field for first-year planting; more timber than you could shake a stick at and fresh meadow close by. And Dedham, too, close enough for aid but not so close as to crowd out newcomers.

Dwight took a last glance across the brook. October sun, sifting through the last red maple leaves, shone on an open patch of ground. He felt a flare of urgency inside. Need, such as he hadn't felt for years. He wanted that land.

* * * * * * *

The members of the survey team finished their journey back to Dedham. They skirted the dry-herd pasture where the rocky woods began and crossed a high plain. Finally, they made their way through the boulder-strewn western edge of the settlement and back to the safety of town.

Timothy must have thought about that land at the crossroads. It was easy land, rich, broad and fertile. Empty. Begging for the touch of a good English plow. That same year, he signed his name with the first proprietors of the new town and pledged with them that land should be apportioned and housing built by summertime of 1651. In fact, he got himself appointed to the committee assigned to lay out house lots for the new village.

Together with John Frairy, Thomas Wight, Robert Hinsdale and Samuel Bullen, Timothy returned to the crossroads in June 1650. Timothy, John and others had already determined the width and layout of the new town's major roads, pinpointing the village center at the crossing of east–west and north–south trails and glorifying the trails as the town's first "highways." The group surveyed a plot for the meetinghouse right at the crossroads. Next to it along the main track was a home lot for Mr. Ralph Wheelock, a highly respected community leader and minister (although he would not lead the Medfield flock). A lot that would be the Reverend Mr. Wilson's was next, then Joshua Fisher's and one for George Barber, who would build the town's mill. John Ellis had a spot on the other side of the meetinghouse lot. All these men had strips of plow land ready cleared, running south of the track, where the old Indian planting field had been. Committee member Samuel Bullen chose a house site along the eastern edge of that fertile, well-drained planting field, and the men also laid out lots for Morse, Allen, Clark, Hamant and Turner bordering that field, which they called the Great Plain.

Other than Bullen, though, the committee members looked across the brook for their own house lots. Another plain extended northward behind the meetinghouse common, sloping only at its southern edge, and gently, at that. There, nudging up against the stream, John Frairy and Timothy Dwight staked out their twelve acres as long, narrow strips. Robert Hinsdale and Thomas Wight ran their lots east–west, facing Medfield's other highway (now North Street).

After the lots were staked out, they had a year to build on land that was free.

John Dwight must have encouraged his brother. It was best for all. John's son, another Timothy, was nearing manhood and would need what influence and property John had to set the boy on his feet. Both brothers knew there was no way in Dedham for Timothy to catch up to John. The land, the power, the respect, even the healthy progeny set John eternally ahead. Not that Timothy wasn't inherently worthy. By 1650, at the age of forty or so, he was proving himself a leader of men, sound in thought on town meeting floor, strong and capable on the training field, knowledgeable of the land and what it offered. But in Dedham he would always be a second comer. Only in a new place might he take his place in the first rank of men.

So the brothers nodded in agreement on the decision. Much of what was thought was left unsaid. But John was quick to buy up Timothy's most valuable Dedham holdings: upland and meadow, mowing and crop land. He bought it for his son to inherit. Timothy sold it all to finance the move, putting all his eggs in the one basket of Medfield. All over Dedham, men were doing the same, selling grant lands in exchange for labor, lumber or the cash they needed to build anew. This was not so expensive a proposition as moving across an ocean, by a long shot, but still, there was housing to be built and fencing to be made, roads to be improved that called for draft animals and equipment as well as a man's bare hands. There were real costs in this land with little money.

Timothy Dwight sold his last Dedham lands in March 1651. The town clerk made a note to himself: "Deed to make for Tho Herring [from] Tymo Dwight one house Lott 6 acres more or less upland & all houses &c. abutts mill Creeke East. John.Dwight & Rich Ellice west. Tho Herring north Joh Dwight south…together wth the purchased Lands & woodeland & wt so ever other Lands Tymo Dwight have now in Dedham unsold." Then he added an unusual postscript, noting that the deed was to be dated July 1, 1651.[11]

A SMALL AHA!

Why was the deed postdated by four months? Because in order to begin his new life sixteen pounds richer, Timothy Dwight was selling the house out from under Mary and himself to his next-door neighbor. And Timothy was willing to do that because he was sure that by the first of July in 1651, a new house would be ready in Medfield, on a special parcel of land he'd helped lay out.

FIRST GENERATION

The western sun was low, raking across the half-cleared field, showing up ragged stumps and exposed roots. It glimmered on the patches of brook not shaded by vines and turned the new roof shingles yellow gold. Welcoming smoke rose from the chimney.

Timothy stopped midstride on the slope above the house just to look. Not a bad piece of work. Bit rough around the edges yet. It'd look a sight better when the summer slow time came and he had space to split and nail up clapboarding. Still, the place was framed in true, and a shingled roof was solid overhead in time for moving day.

Pity it was so small—more like a crofter's hut than a manor house by Woolverstone standards. But then, their house was none smaller than those of many worthy men. Later, there'd be time to add on. Yet how much adding was called for, after all, with just the two of them? Maybe a nephew now and then, borrowed for haying or harvesting. No Dwights to come from this house surely, what with Mary well past bearing. Not that he didn't have a flicker or two left in him. Forty-odd was young enough and then some. He felt an ache

deep inside that he couldn't assign for sure to gut or groin. Timothy scowled to make it go away and went back to considering.

He'd built the hall big enough for what needed doing indoors. Mary had plenty of hearth room for baking and the eternal pot of broth simmering to the side. Someone always needed her tending. No scrimping on storeroom neither—a whole great room above stairs. Of course, he admitted quietly, he'd almost had to do that, seeing how close the groundwater flowed to the surface. Who could have known, when they'd laid out the home lots? All those little trickles of water flowing invisible downslope to the brook. Made something of a mess of the cellar the workmen had dug. They ended up settling for a space so shallow Timothy couldn't even stand. But Mary could get down there, when need be, and it'd keep the cheese cool in summer and the roots from freezing in winter.

He turned his back on the raw new building and pushed up the brim of his hat. Groundwater or no, this was the right spot. Just enough trees here to shade the house in summer, the house that faced south and that would, come wintertime, soak up the low sun through leafless branches. And he liked the sound of the brook, just as he had in Dedham.

John Frairy had felt the same, building his own house cheek-by-jowl with Dwight's. And just across the fording place in the brook, the meetinghouse would be raising soon, with more houses ranging eastward along the high road. Mister Wheelock, Joshua Fisher and others—the worthiest men in Medfield—were working just like him, splitting shingles and fencing their dooryards, getting their first crops in and turning a crossroads into a town.

Timothy watched the water sparkle where it slipped over rocks in the stream. The little house and its twelve-acre plot behind him was just a beginning. Hard work and the grace of God would see this Dwight a rich man yet—though whose riches they would be when he was gone didn't bear thinking on.

* * * * *

Dwight had little enough time to think on the future during those first years, when so much was happening in the present. The new village immediately elected him one of its selectmen. He continued to serve in that capacity for eleven of the next fifteen years, although the number of selectmen appears to have varied from one year to the next.[12] The men who served with him were Medfield's community leaders, whose names recur in the records throughout this first generation: Wheelock, Wight, Frairy and Hinsdale, joined in time by Clark and Adams.

It was not surprising that Timothy was among Medfield's political leaders. He began as a high-ranked original member of the community, and both his wealth and prestige grew in the decades that followed. In that first year of 1652, a property valuation was made for each of the town's proprietors. Timothy ranked third highest in the town: Wight, Frairy, Dwight, Wheelock, Morse—the town fathers.

Much was expected from those to whom much was given. Timothy, a twelve-acre householder, had to put the services of an ox team, as well as his own labor, to work on improving the town's roads. "Brother Dwight" and "brother Wight" were charged with building a town pound behind the meetinghouse between their two properties. Forty by forty feet square and six rails high, the pound for stray animals was larger than the meetinghouse itself.[13]

Timothy was elected Medfield's first deputy to the colony's General Court. He met monthly with the selectmen to manage the town's business, set tax rates and establish a body of regulations to maintain order. Not that those regulations were all so new or different from those of other towns. Fences had to be built three feet, six inches high. (Dedham's similar regulation was included in its town covenant.) Hogs had to be ringed—secured by a nose ring—at all times (earlier, Hingham had tried to require this only during planting season, but the hogs had caused so much field damage at other seasons that they were permanently restrained).

Selectmen supervised (and, we might assume, arbitrated) any division of common lands that had been approved at town meeting. They apportioned meadow lots along the Charles River. They laid out the South Plain, which would become one of Medfield's longest used planting fields, in strips of up to twenty acres per person. They negotiated with the colonial government for additional land west of the Charles to be added to the town, and when this was approved, they oversaw the division of this New Grant among town residents.

Dwight received 146 acres in the division, plus 20 at South Plain and 21 in the Charles River meadows. All told, by the time of his death he had accumulated approximately 305 acres of land in present-day Medfield, Millis, Medway and Norfolk.[14] While some of the land was left "unimproved"—an investment like the New Grant acres—other parcels required varying amounts of attention and hard labor. Most intensively worked was Dwight's home lot, the twelve acres on which he built a house and barn, as well as a pigsty, livestock sheds and one or more pens. He planted, pruned and harvested an orchard on part of that land, and cleared and plowed the rest for planting vegetables, flax and the generic "pease" (legumes) that always show up in valuation and inventory lists. Undoubtedly Timothy Dwight did not accomplish all this work single-handedly. He had the wherewithal to hire help during the eight-month farm season and the respectability to offer what amounted to resident training in husbandry to young sons of relatives and friends.[15]

Besides his home lot garden, Dwight also owned "a parcell of land lying in the field in the middle of ye town." Whether this was the South Plain division land or a smaller plot in the original planting fields, this land was for grain crops. Come spring every year, the soil needed turning and planting to Indian corn, wheat, rye and oats.[16] A month later, corn was "half-hilled"—the soil built up around the growing stalks for support. When another month had gone by, the process was repeated.

Meanwhile, the hay on Dwight's twenty-nine acres of river meadow ripened and had to be scythed and stacked on high spots in the swamp, there to begin drying and wait for the river to recede in summer's drought. It was then possible to load the hay on barges, pole the high-heaped load to a landing place and transfer it to a hay wain for transport to the home farm. Here the advantage of natural grasslands broke down. Barge transport involved four separate loading operations, as well as reliance on a river that could flood or run so shallow as to threaten even shallow-bottomed barges with grounding.

By 1660, Dwight was impatient with water transport. He constructed a cart bridge across the Charles from his meadows on the west side and then received permission to lay out a road to "Dwight's Bridge" "for convenience of access to his meadows." What Dwight had in mind was not just any road. It was a road that cut across extensive meadow lots on the river's east side. He had to avoid damaging the meadow lots, and he had to build the road across a swamp.

Evidence of watery roads in other towns suggests that Dwight's cart path may not have been designed for year-round use.[17] Since its purpose was access to hay, which was only harvested in summer months at time of low water, Dwight may have settled for clearing a swath through riverside brush, carting in rocks and gravel where necessary to make a solid bottom and letting the roadway sit under water during the wet season. However he achieved his goal, he convinced the town that the road was worthwhile, for

Dwight's causeway to the meadows, raised high after three hundred years of use.

town meeting vote the following year made "Dwights causey" (causeway) a town way. Today, dozens of layers of gravel later, Dwight Street still follows the route that Timothy laid out across the meadow in 1660. No longer in public use, it leads to the concrete abutments of a later Dwight's Bridge, washed out during the 1938 hurricane.[18]

Timothy Dwight was an achiever. The effort that he could not put into raising children, he instead put into his land and the town around him. He was Medfield's "lieutenant," appointed by the General Court to be in charge of military training and preparedness for the town. He was one of the select committee chosen to assign seats in the meetinghouse—a delicate task that resulted in a highly visible rank ordering of every family in the town.

Another form of rank ordering appears in the valuation lists that formed the basis for apportioning taxes. In a situation surprisingly reminiscent of present-day Medfield, revaluation of a man's estate was required frequently as the number of town residents was growing, and the acreage owned by each family changed with every distribution of town land. A valuation done in 1660, nine years after Medfield's founding, provides the occasion for a closer look at Timothy Dwight and his neighbors.

The men who first settled in Medfield and occupied the center of town were generally also the town's wealthiest residents. Thus, the valuation list is—not coincidentally—a list of both wealth and neighborhood, at least at the top.

John Thurston	£281	5 sons; one living next door
Thomas Wight	£266	4 sons living; 1 in Dedham, 1 next door
John Frairy Jr.	£264	(married Abraham Harding's widow)
John Frairy Sr.	£252	4 sons; 1 in Boston, 3 in Medfield
Henry Smith	£251	5 sons; 1 in Dedham
Timothy Dwight	£242	no children
Robert Hinsdale	£241	6 sons; most to Connecticut Valley in 1660s
Henry Adams	£197	5 sons at home; owns 250 acres in Sherborn
Ralph Wheelock	£190	4 sons in town

In this top-ranking hierarchy, Timothy Dwight stands out for one reason alone: he is a childless man. This was a situation with far-reaching implications for his valued estate. Under normal circumstances, a father in seventeenth-century Massachusetts would divide his property among his heirs: one portion to each son, up to one portion to the husband of each daughter, with a double portion going to the eldest male heir. Were this to happen to even these wealthiest Medfield landowners, the heirs would not inherit a comfortable living: a father with three hundred acres of land had only one hundred acres to leave to his eldest son and fifty to younger ones, at a time when sixty to one hundred acres were estimated to be needed for subsistence farming.

There were compensating circumstances. One or more children might move on to the next rank of new settlements, as the Hinsdales chose to do, there to get their own sizable land grants as early proprietors. The portion of Medfield land given them by their father would be sold to finance the move, just as Timothy Dwight had sold his Dedham land to move to Medfield. The land for sale would be bought by another second-generation son looking to enlarge his farm. Moreover, when a young man married—an event frequently concurrent with setting up on his own—he would receive his bride's marriage portion to supplement his own patrimony. Chances were good, then, that the second generation would do well in an agricultural society, and even the third generation, in many cases. But it must have been clear even to these first settlers that the process could not succeed indefinitely, and that their sons or grandsons would be forced to revert to the English inheritance system of primogeniture that they had attempted to leave behind.[19]

Clearly, Timothy Dwight need not be concerned about apportioning his 305 acres. Were he one to put a good face on his childless condition, he would consider the advantage he could leave to his nephews, or even his grandnephews in Dedham, since John Dwight's son, Timothy's namesake and his six successive wives were producing an inexhaustible supply of children.[20] Still, it must have been difficult to put away regrets entirely, assigning them to God's will. Timothy Dwight had succeeded beyond the wildest of English dreams, building a patrimony to be proud of, but he had no one, down the years, to work the land with or leave it to.

* * * * * * *

The year 1668 must have seemed the nadir of Timothy's life, a time to lose himself in purifying prayer or sweat-filled days. As the year began, Mary Dwight died. She had lived through seventy-four years of hard labor, changes and disappointments, thirty-four of them as Timothy's wife.

Come town meeting in the spring, Dwight was not elected to his customary office of selectman—or did he refuse the position? A rumble of discontent was running through Medfield as town meeting members discussed limiting the selectmen's decision-making powers. A number of people disagreed, particularly members of the old guard, including the Reverends Wilson and Wheelock, John Frairy "and some others." Certainly, Dwight was part of the old guard, and his removal from the board of selectmen, whether by vote or choice, would have reinforced the man's sense that his time was over.

In May, the colony records indicate that "Timo Dwight, on acct. of defective eyesight, and at his own request, is discharged from further duty as leftenant at Medfield."[21] Dwight was verging on sixty. What part his wife's death had in his decision to withdraw from public life is a matter of speculation. The combined effect of Mary's death and the removal of Dwight's political and military responsibilities, however, must have meant, at the very least, that he spent many more silent nights and solitary daytime hours than he was used to.

What happened next was thoroughly unpredictable. Perhaps it came from Dwight's travels to Boston—on his own business maybe, or in earlier years on the town's business. He would have ridden through Dedham, stopping at the old house to visit with his brother's widow (John Dwight had died in 1661) or a nephew's family. From there he would cross over Mother Brook and follow one of the winding roads toward Boston, past farms spread some distance apart, eleven miles as the crow flies but a lot longer and slower as the road meandered. Along the way, the horse would need watering. Perhaps he stopped at John Watson's Roxbury farm, located in a valley later described as a "very forbidding district."[22] Likely the Watsons and the Dwights knew one another, John Watson being another first comer and the same age as John Dwight.

Whatever the sequence of events and considerations leading up to July 8, 1669, on that date John and Alice Watson's daughter, Dorcas, married Timothy Dwight in Medfield. She was thirty years old. His life was never the same. Twelve months later, Dorcas gave birth to Timothy Dwight Jr. That same year, Dwight was returned to the board of selectmen. He added to his acreage through another common land division. A year later, he and Dorcas became eighty pounds richer when elderly John Watson died. Within six months, a second son, John Dwight, was born, but he died the next winter. In May 1675, a third son, also named John, was born.

The house that Timothy and Mary Dwight had shared for twenty years must suddenly have seemed very cramped, what with cradle, trundle bed, crawling babies and a second dower chest of goods. It was probably also old-fashioned by 1675, for Timothy had not made any attempt to enlarge it to more appropriately reflect his standing in the community. For twenty years he and John Frairy, living side by side, had apparently settled for similar small, basic houses.

No direct evidence of what Dwight's first home must have been like, other than a few ancient timbers, still remains within the present building. John Frairy, however, never did add on to his house, so the inventory taken of Frairy's possessions when he died in 1675 provides a plausible comparison to the condition of Dwight's house. It had a cellar for storage; a single ground-floor room that was hall, parlor, cooking and living all in one; and a chamber above crammed full of bedding and furniture. It was very crowded.[23]

Aha! Moment: Lamb's Tongues and Mold

The town did Save This House, as the Medfield Day banner had insisted, in 1996. It went before town meeting and the purchase was approved, against the better judgment of the selectmen, who were (reasonably) worried about potential drain on the municipal treasury caused by ownership of a pink elephant.

A year later, the house was still pink, still decrepit. The windows were boarded up to discourage human intruders and the chimney wrapped in blue tarp to discourage four-footed ones. Whenever it rained, the cellar still flooded, including the concrete moat where the furnace sat (a moat built, undoubtedly, to keep water out, but more effective at keeping it in). Except for the stream that flowed regularly from back to front through the cellar, there was no running water, as the pipes had frozen. But the Friends of the Dwight-Derby House had been incorporated, and a lot was about to happen.

The Friends had convinced the Board of Selectmen to lease the house to them indefinitely, in exchange for promising to put the building into usable condition and manage the uses it would have. There were advantages to this arrangement. The town was absolved of fiscal responsibility for what promised to be exorbitant restoration costs. The Friends could apply for private nonprofit project funding. They could also build a board of people guaranteed to put the good of the house ahead of a number of other "goods" that might be proposed.

Behind the plywood and under the tarp, the house was being scrutinized. Informal walk-throughs by old house experts[24] segued into a study tour by the Vernacular Architecture Forum and, finally, a formal "historic structures report" written by The Preservation Cooperative (TPC), with input from Lawrence Sorli. Larry and the Cooperative's Mary Turkel and Bob Majors were architectural historians used to looking at buildings that were more than they first appeared.

Being used to looking and understanding what you see are not synonymous. A fly on the wall could hear a lot of visions and revisions as Mary, Bob and Larry wandered from room to room. They spent some time wading in the cellar (Mary's allergies discovered the mold and mildew; Larry's head discovered bug-eaten beams), but the foundation didn't offer much historic information except an undatable sequence of enlargements and, at some point, cement packed in between the dry laid fieldstones—a vain effort to divert the perennial cellar stream.

On the ground floor, the east front parlor—the room that caused all the original excitement, with its chamfered beams, lamb's tongue stops and raised sill—and the room directly over it (dubbed the "parlor chamber," as in John Frairy's house) were the only finished rooms that clearly dated from the seventeenth century, Timothy Dwight's era or maybe, at the latest, his son John's. The west front rooms were definitely later, probably mid-1700s. But there was a glitch. The old kitchen, with its no later than 1700 bake oven tucked at the rear of a massive cooking hearth, backed up against *both* east and west side parlors. The common chimney, in other words, had to be earlier than the apparent date of the west rooms. Mary and Bob and Larry headed for the attic.

The attic, full of that dry musty smell that attics are supposed to have, was also full of information, for those who knew where to look. An architectural tour of the Dwight-Derby House could begin and end in the attic without

Chamfered summer beam with lamb's tongue stop, east parlor.

missing a single significant change in the building's history. The three specialists examined the beams that framed in the puzzling common chimney and discovered rafter notches where no rafters exist. They looked between the beams and saw pieces of vertical posts where there was no structural reason to have any. They found dozens of other clues and surprises, but these two were enough to send Bob for his pry bar.

In the second-floor hallway, there is a jog at the bottom of the attic stairs. Two broad vertical boards box in the corner. Bob, carefully easing the dry boards out to avoid splitting, exposed what was behind them. Illuminated in the beam of a strong flashlight was a hodgepodge of ancient timbers. One vertical post pinned into a massive carrying beam. Another post was roughly chopped off. Behind what looked like the main beam, another, equal in size, was visible. An assortment of other pieces, including one with a slant-cut end, all jockeyed for space, puzzling the uninitiated and challenging the experts.

Two visits and much discussion later, Larry and TPC reached an explanation they could agree on that conformed to all the obscure pieces of evidence and illuminated a moment of change in Dwight-Derby House history.

When Timothy Dwight needed more room, he decided to double the size of his house, building two more rooms on the opposite side of the end chimney, which would become a central chimney. The addition was effectively self-contained, butting up against the original structure. Probably it included a low-beamed full cellar. In order to keep the original roof intact while the builder worked—and in accordance with prevailing fashion—the roof of the addition was built at right angles to the original. Finally, when the new part was weather-tight, new fireplaces could be tied in to the main chimney, the two roofs could be connected and interior doors cut through. Dorcas Dwight had room to work and the boys had room to run. In due course, Timothy and Dorcas would expect to retire to the new part, in accordance with tradition, while a son's young family made do in the older rooms until it all became theirs.[25]

"IF IT SHALL PLEASE GOD THAT THEY STAND"

"Neat and trim, Master Metcalf. Neat and trim."

"You've doubts about the matter, Master Dwight?" The square-built carpenter glanced up from his plane just long enough to raise a quizzical eyebrow. Then he went back to the perfect edge he was carving, the length of a massive timber.

"Nay, nay, Michael. You know as well as I, my regard for your skill. But it's for the mistress, now, isn't it? Neat and trim for the new Mistress Dwight."

An unaccustomed lightness in Dwight's tone, Michael noted.

"A building to match the bride then."

"Aye."

Michael Metcalf traded plane for gouge and turned his attention to one end of the beam, where he'd stopped cutting the chamfer. Lightly, delicately, he knocked a chip out of the oak, then another. Repositioning the sharp blade, he chipped more slivers off the edge until a gentle, undulating curve took shape. It seemed to rise up from the hollow where the chip had been and then slide down toward the end of the beam, a wave cresting and stretching out toward the shore. Timothy Dwight watched silently, leery of distracting him.

The housewright finally eased back on his haunches and then walked the length of the twelve-foot timber that lay alongside others in the yard. He calmly ignored Dwight's supervision as he began to repeat his series of cuts.

The older man spoke up. "Never could see where those stops came by their name. Always looked like ocean waves to me."

Metcalf was already engrossed in the next carving.

"Lamb's tongues, Master Dwight." He paused and glanced up, and gouge became pointer, sketching the straight chamfer line along the timber's edge, sweeping briefly up, then gracefully down again in the curve that was a traditional finish. "Sure you can see the little lamb's tongue, having just licked his mam's teat clean."

Dwight nodded, a glimmer of amusement shining through the film beginning to obscure his right eye.

"Ah, but it was the waves that brought me here, Master Metcalf. The waves and Almighty God."

"Amen to them both."

Metcalf watched Dwight stride off toward the barn, strength still in every step, belying his three-score years. And an air about him spoke of the years he'd run the town. Dwight and Wight, Adams and Wheelock. The Reverend Mister Wilson, of course. The power that ran Medfield. As for himself, there was pride in following the trade the Metcalfs knew as well as any hereabouts. And if it was hard work, he still gave thanks to the Lord for the benefits to be won.

Dwight's passage toward the barn was filled with memories. Broad fields dotted with grazing sheep. The pebble textured flint walls of St. Dunstan's. A dust-filled high road winding between Burstall's half-timbered houses where Mary Lotten lived .The memories moved on to the waves he'd envisioned just now. Taut sails and numb faces of October on the ocean. A discreet touch to his wife's hand as they stood by one another at the rail, staring out toward what they could not see, knowing whatever hope they had for better had to lie ahead.

He nearly tripped over a chipped old pan that Dorcas had set out to water the hens. Dwight snorted in disgust at himself and picked up his pace, turning his head more to make full use of the good eye.

* * * * * *

New family, new house, new lease on life. Timothy Dwight was doing well at the age of sixty-six. Life was not so promising for others, however, in 1675. Conflict with Indians, especially the Wampanoag and Nipmuc tribes, was becoming more frequent and more violent by the month. Nearby, as early as 1672, a Natick Indian named John Awashamog had taken exception to the colony's grant of land in the Sherborn area to Medfield. Awashamog, having developed a sophisticated understanding of the differing Indian and English concepts of "ownership," claimed that the New Grant lands west of the Charles River were his. Medfield, conscious of the rising hostility among English and local tribes, lost no time appointing a committee whose negotiations resulted in payment to Awashamog of twenty-one pounds, four shillings for the multithousand-acre area.

By 1675, even this financial diplomacy was not sufficient to avert hostilities. Swansea, Rehoboth, Taunton, Middleborough, Dartmouth and Mendon to the southeast, followed by half a dozen towns to the west, were attacked. Medfield made sure it had a new militia leader to replace Dwight: Henry Adams, the miller, took on the position, along with representing Medfield in the General Court. Adams laid in a stock of powder and ammunition for the town and oversaw the purchase of a cannon—useful especially as a signal gun in case of emergency.

But town affairs were not limited to defensive actions in the face of an uncertain danger. Too many threats and alarms in the past had come to nothing for the present one to halt Medfield's internal workings. In 1675, Timothy Dwight was once again off the board of selectmen. Thomas Wight, with whom he had served during much of his tenure, had died the previous year. New and slightly younger names appeared in town government: John Harding (stepson of John Frairy Jr.), John Ellis (whose house stood just south of Dwight's across the brook) and John Metcalf were the only named selectmen that year. Town meeting voted to parcel out another six hundred acres of town land to its seventy-seven proprietors. A subscription for funds to build a new, brick college at Cambridge had Dwight down for a ten-shilling cash donation—this in contrast to most subscribers, who pledged bushels of corn or, rarely, wheat.[26]

Other aspects of life in Medfield had permanently changed by 1675. As Dwight was congratulating himself on his good fortune and family to uphold his name in Medfield, many of the men who had formed the original settlement cohort found themselves less fortunate. A glance at the nine men with whom Dwight was ranked, and who were his closest neighbors fifteen years earlier, shows a social evolution taking place in the town.

- John Thurston: three married sons still in town, one in Boston, one on Long Island. By 1740, the last family member had left Medfield.
- Thomas Wight: died 1674; one son in Dedham; one on homestead; two burned out 1676 but rebuilt in Medfield.
- John Frairy Jr.: died 1670; no children.
- John Frairy Sr.: died 1675; one son in Boston, two in Connecticut Valley.
- Henry Smith: three sons married and living in Medfield, two dead. At least one Smith line would remain in Medfield through the nineteenth century.
- Robert Hinsdale: most of this family moved to the Connecticut Valley in the 1660s. Robert and four of his sons were killed during King Philip's War; one son died in Medfield without an heir.
- Henry Adams: killed 1676; five sons and their heirs remained in Medfield/Sherborn.
- Ralph Wheelock: four married sons remained in town; descendants here through eighteenth century.

Of the forty-one males in this group who lived in Medfield in 1660, only twenty-two—plus Timothy Dwight's two boys—remained by the end of 1676. Those who remained had a little more land to go around.

Meanwhile, Dorcas Dwight must have sought out her own group of new friends. Being thirty years younger than her husband, she would look to a second generation of Medfield wives for companionship, although many families in town were between generations just then, with children grown but not yet married. Rachel Hinsdale, Gamaliel's wife, may have been sociable, or Lydia Morse, who had married Ephraim Wight the same year Dorcas and Timothy were wed. Lydia Wight was a near neighbor, living in her father-in-law's house on North Street. She and Dorcas shared pregnancies as well as neighborhood, both giving birth in 1670, 1672 and 1675.

But between John Dwight's birth in 1675 and the end of 1676 was to come a major turning point in New England's history—and with it, the history of Medfield and the house on Frairy Street.

On February 19, 1676, a raiding band of Wampanoag attacked the eastern edge of the town, possibly at the same time that another raid began from the river's edge. In the course of a few hours, nearly half the houses in

Medfield, all around the outskirts of the village, were destroyed. Barns full of winter stores of grain and hay, sheds with the livestock penned in them out of the cold, the town's grist- and sawmills, its bridge across the Charles—all burned. Five Medfield men, one woman and four children were killed that day.[27] Three more would die later, one from an accidental shot. Two were wounded and never healed: Daniel Clark and Timothy Dwight.

"Mortally wounded by ye Indians," it was recorded. What was Timothy doing the morning when all hell broke loose? Nothing was burning in the vicinity of his house or the vacant John Frairy house next door. Evidence has the raiding party attacking along the edges of the settlement, as none of the center village buildings was destroyed. Perhaps it was something as simple as needing to know what was going on outside his shuttered house. Perhaps he grabbed the "armes & ammunition" that would be listed in his estate inventory and headed toward the action, an automatic response after years of militia training. Perhaps, knowing that Lieutenant Adams was a distance away at his house by the mill—though not knowing that Adams was lying dead in the doorway—Timothy Dwight stood guard by the "greate Gune" at the meetinghouse and fired it in warning. The second shot, so the story goes, panicked the Indians and they retreated west across the river. But those who had been on the east side of Medfield had to pass through the village on their way, staying close to outbuildings, to the walls of the town pound or to the shade trees and brush along the brook. Timothy, with his "defective eyesight," would have been no match for a hastily aimed arrow or gunshot.

Two weeks later, he was still hanging on to the life that had come to mean so much. He dictated a will, so weak that he could do no more than verify it with a "T" and his seal. He had had time to collect his thoughts during the long bedridden days, and although his faith in the hereafter remained unshaken, his fears for the world around him, the life he had made and the wife whom he treasured are clear in his words:

> *In the name of God Amen Anno Domini 1675/76 March*
> *3^d^ I Timothy Dwight of the Town of Meadfeild*
> *in the County of Suffolk aged about Sixty-Seven*
> *years being sensible of my mortall condition especially*
> *being sorely wounded & not knowing how the Lord*
> *will deale with mee in lengthening out my days*
> *or calling mee home suddenly unto himselfe I doe*
> *therefore thinke it meet to set my house in order*
> *that there may bee no distractions afterward.*

He assigned his soul to God and his body to the earth:

> *Item I will that my whole Estate shalbe divided into four parts: namely a double portion unto Timothy my eldest Son and the rest equally in single portions and parts to my most beloved wife Dorcas Dwight, and John my younger Son. Item my will and testament is that my Son Timothy shall have the house and barn if it shall please God that they stand…*
> *Item. my will is that my beloved wife shalbe at her liberty to choose an Over Seer to assist her about my Estate*[28]

On March 9, 1676, Timothy Dwight died.

Interval

Timothy left a young family with an ailing child in the middle of wartime.[29] But unlike many other Medfield families, the Dwights were neither homeless nor impoverished, and they had a wide safety net of family support in neighboring towns. It is hard to imagine what Dorcas Dwight endured in those first late winter weeks after Timothy's death. She may have taken her sons to Dedham to stay with Dwight kin there. An inventory of the deceased man's possessions, taken a year after his death, includes "Goods prised [appraised] at Dedham," which consisted solely of linens—mostly bedding—that could well have been from Dorcas's dower chest.

War and death notwithstanding, there was still a whole farm to run in Medfield, however that could be managed. Timothy Dwight's will names his wife executrix of the estate—a fairly unusual choice that speaks to his trust in her judgment. He also provides her additional support to accomplish the constant work demanded of a farmer: "my beloved wife shalbe at her liberty to choose an Over Seer to assist her about my Estate and disposition of it as Shee shall like."[30] Dorcas found an "Over Seer" among the Medfield men. It is worth speculating that Edward Adams, a contemporary of her husband who witnessed his will, may have referred her to his nephew John for the position. John would appear in the documentary record a year after Timothy's death.

Three days before the first anniversary of Timothy Dwight's death, the Widow Dwight invited into her Medfield home three respectable local men to make a "true Inventory" of all of Timothy Dwight's possessions and appraise their value so that they could be distributed among the heirs. This one-year hiatus between death and distribution was common, a year being the normal period of full mourning for the deceased.

The appraisers did not find a closed house and an abandoned farm. There were two colts in the barn, along with twenty-six other assorted livestock and a team of oxen. Fifteen bushels of corn, plus wheat, rye, "pease" and oats probably stood in sacks in the storeroom, and there were "other provisions in the house" as well. The carefully itemized inventory testifies to Timothy Dwight's worldly success as no other document could. He owned 340 acres of land in three different towns. His home lot included a "dwelling house barn & Orchard." The barn, of which no evidence remained by the twentieth century, was likely a combined-use livestock and grain barn, one part of which included a threshing floor where Dwight's wheat and rye were processed. It would have been located near the house for ease of access, but far enough distant to prevent an all-too-common barn fire from spreading to the house.[31] Two broodmares stood in his barn, as well as the ox team, suggesting that the horses were riding animals. Fifty pounds—one tenth of his total estate—was in cash or debts due. This was essentially surplus cash, which Dwight had invested by making loans to neighbors or kinsmen in this era before banks.

Dwight's "indoor movables" did not add up to a luxurious lifestyle. As was common among rural landowners, his wealth was in land, not possessions, but still, the four-room house was comfortably furnished by seventeenth-century standards. The downstairs best room, or parlor, held three beds (one "small") and a number of showy items like pewter plates and a silver cup. Upstairs, the "parler chamber" held another bed, as well as an assortment of chairs and stools, a spinning wheel and a cradle. This room faced southeast and was warm in the winter, overlooking the town brook and the meetinghouse. It would have made a good sitting room, especially in the morning. The kitchen, in the old section of the house, was predictably crammed with furnishings and utensils: bedstead, cupboard, spinning wheel, small worktable, long table with benches and stools, "one frying pan, tramel & other utensils about ye fire." The older upstairs room seems to have been a storeroom for foodstuffs and unused linens, where they would stay dry and relatively safe from mice and squirrels.[32]

All told, the appraisers valued Timothy Dwight's estate at £507, 7 shillings and sixpence. Dwight's wish had been that what he owned be traditionally divided in fourths: one fourth for his wife's use until she died or remarried, one fourth for baby John and two fourths for Timothy, the eldest son. But Timothy did not survive to adulthood, and Dorcas, on May 8, 1677, married John Adams, her Medfield neighbor. Two-year-old John Dwight became heir to one of the largest estates in the town.

* * * * * * *

Nothing probably changed much over the next twenty years, at least in the Dwight-Adams household. Young John walked across North Street to school for a few weeks each year. Stepfather Adams—a much younger man than the father whom John had never known—taught him how to manage the great farm that would all be his when he reached his majority. John Adams's own father died in 1690, leaving land on Bridge Street and elsewhere to his son, as well as part interest in the family house that had been rebuilt after King Philip's War.[33] This was the first time that Adams had actually owned his own land, having worked the Dwight estate for the fourteen years since his marriage to Dorcas.

* * * * * * *

On December 3, 1696, seven months after his twenty-first birthday, John Dwight married Elizabeth Harding in Dedham.[34] The Hardings were another old Medfield family who had been neighbors of the Adamses on Bridge Street until they too were burned out during the war and relocated to present-day Harding Street.

That same year, the town had decided to get rid of old John Frairy's house. Frairy's property, next door to the Dwights, had been donated to Medfield by his son, who had a prosperous business in Boston. Income from the parcel was to be used to support education and the ministry, so over the years, the lot had been rented out for haying and, presumably, for its apple harvest, since one visitor to town specifically referred to "the orchard that Mr. Frairy had given."[35] In 1696, the town voted to sell the original Frairy house, "all excepting brick and clay" (not easily recyclable), and use the cash to pay for fencing the twelve-acre parcel abutting Dwight's. The fenced land could then be leased as pasture, which brought higher rents than hayfields and was thus more profitable for the town.

Frairy's 1652 house could not have been in good condition by 1696, especially if it had been empty for twenty years. Many of its hand-hewn beams, floorboards and clapboards could be salvaged, however, and reused as building material on another site. Regrettably, the version of town records that still exists did not record who bought the Frairy place. It may well have been John Dwight, about to embark on his own building campaign at the house that remained on Frairy Street.

Off the back of the wide rectangular house, Dwight built his wife a new kitchen. The addition was one story high with a shed roof that pinned into the main house below second-story windows. It didn't stretch all the way to the east end because an exterior door at the back was too useful to cover up. It did line up with the west wall, though, and provided room for a small chamber there, close to the heart of family activity (the so-called "borning room" of Colonial Revival fame); probably a matching small cool room at the northeast side used as a milk room;[36] and a big central work space dominated by an eight-foot-wide hearth. The hearth allowed Elizabeth to keep a cooking fire going on one side, while she also used the bake oven set back into the chimney.

It was a kitchen big enough for a family to crowd into during frigid winter days; a good kitchen in summer as well (for all except the cooks) because it could be closed off from other first-floor space. As an added benefit, it was no longer necessary to cook in the old front room of the house. The Dwights had effectively added new parlor space or, more likely, new bedchamber space for some of the seven children to come.

* * * * * * *

The years of John and Elizabeth's marriage project through history as a remarkably quiet interlude. At one end were the shouts and groans of Timothy Dwight's nascent America. At the other was the rumble of Seth and Hannah's empire crumbling in a small, private revolution coinciding with that of the country at large. From the time of John Dwight's marriage in 1696 to his death in 1751, his voice is barely heard in the records. Late in life, he served as town clerk and then briefly as Medfield's representative to the General Court, but there was never the constant public presence that typified his father's life. John Dwight chose a small bit part in the progress of Medfield's and the colony's history.

Part of this may have been due simply to the relative calm that characterized the town's development during John's lifetime. Medfield, having survived and recovered from the 1676 attack, went about the business of securing its place in the New World. It was a generation of accrual, of building on what had come before. Families across eastern Massachusetts were institutionalizing the estate, the status, the family line that, for Timothy Dwight and his wives, had been more dream than reality. Town records reflect an absorption with local affairs: meetinghouses and ministers' pay; boundary disputes and the loss of Medway; protection of the town's natural resources of wood and meadow hay; the laying out of roads that reached to farmsteads and mills near the borders. The witchcraft hysteria that devastated society in North Shore towns apparently did not deeply affect Medfield. The series of colonial wars that continued to disrupt the peace of other communities claimed the lives of only three Medfield men in fifty years. The one dramatic event that stirred Medfield's inhabitants in John's lifetime was the Great Awakening—a period of widespread religious revival and controversy in the 1730s and '40s—although the presence of the revered Reverend Mr. Baxter in the Medfield pulpit seems to have kept controversy to a minimum and the congregation growing.

The recorded silence of John Dwight in no way implies that he sat still. In fact, all the energy that he had inherited from Timothy was channeled into private life. John was master of a five-hundred-acre estate, much of which was still unimproved land. He was *pater familias* for seven children born between 1698 and 1716, five of them girls who, while they may have eased Elizabeth's constant workload, would not have helped much with the estate management. There were few domestic crises in the Dwight family—or at least, if there were, they are invisible from this distance. Timothy, their teenage son, died in November 1715; the cause of his death was unrecorded. The family, John in particular, must have been devastated by the loss of his only son, the expected heir to the Dwight homestead.

But just a year later, thirty-eight-year-old Elizabeth gave birth to one last child. Seth Dwight was born on November 16, 1716. He would grow up, like his father before him, surrounded by his patrimony, living every day secure in the knowledge that house, land and social place were his.

In a pattern familiar to colonial families, Seth, the youngest, remained in his parents' home as a single man well into adulthood. He worked for his father, learned the skills of agriculture and animal husbandry and came to know intimately every parcel of the family land. Along the way, he proved to his parents that he belonged to the land and that he would take care of it. Did his mother finally give him a nudge toward matrimony? Did his father speak to him about carrying on the family name? Did Seth simply get to know Hannah Fisher as he worked on the land his father owned near her family's farm?[37] Whatever the impetus, Seth Dwight became engaged to

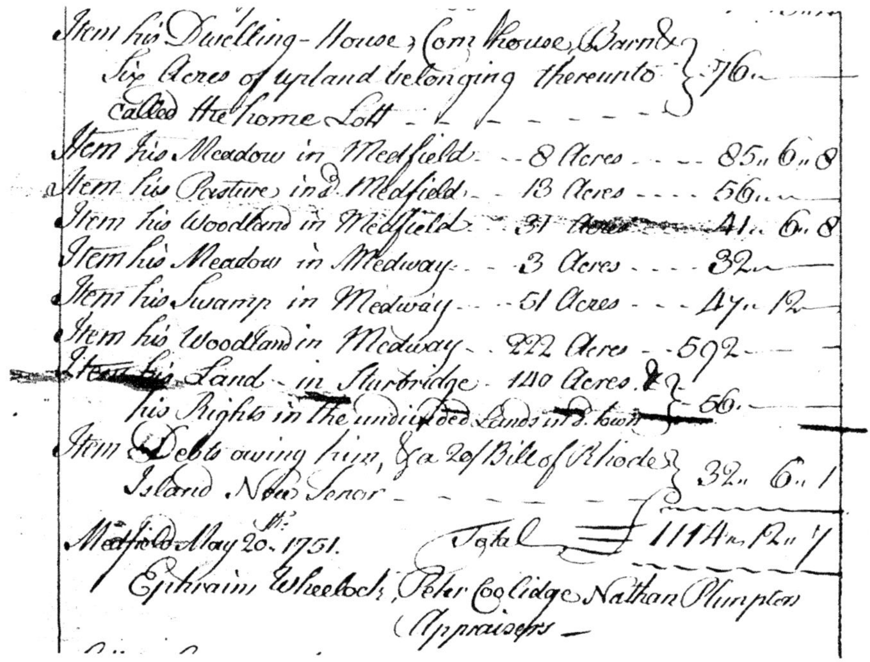
Item his Dwelling-House, Corn House, Barn & Six Acres of upland belonging thereunto called the home Lott — 76..
Item his Meadow in Medfield — 8 Acres — 85.. 6.. 8
Item his Pasture in Medfield — 13 Acres — 56..
Item his Woodland in Medfield — 31 Acres — 41.. 6.. 8
Item his Meadow in Medway — 3 Acres — 32..
Item his Swamp in Medway — 51 Acres — 47.. 12
Item his Woodland in Medway — 222 Acres — 592
Item his Land in Sturbridge 140 Acres & his Rights in the undivided Lands in d. town — 56.
Item Debts owing him, & a 20/ Bill of Rhode Island New Tenor — 32.. 6.. 1
Medfield May 20th 1751. Total £1114.. 12.. 7
Ephraim Wheelock, Peter Coolidge, Nathan Plimpton Appraisers

Part of John Dwight's 1751 probate inventory, including "house, corn barn, barn and… home lott." *Suffolk Register of Probate.*

Hannah Fisher, and two weeks before the wedding, John Dwight presented them with their wedding present. It was couched in the form of a deed of sale, with Seth nominally putting up £650 for the property.[38] In practical terms, however, it was a gift from one generation to the next, securing the family line and its estate for the foreseeable future.

> *Know ye that I, John Dwight of Medfield*
> *Give Grant Bargain Sell Aliene Convey and Confirm unto* [Seth Dwight]
> *…The One half of my House being the East End, and also the one half of my Barn and*
> *Barn yards and Gardens, and also the One half of my Orchard.*
> *and more also Six acres of Upland lying in my Home Lot…*
> *And also…a tract of pasture land 7½ acres by estimate…*
> *a tract of meadow land 10 acres by estimation allowing a Cart Way*
> *through my own Meadow where the Causey now is…*
> *47 acres by estimation abutted North on Natick line.*

> *In witness whereof I have hereunto set my Hand and Seal this Twenty fifth Day of November Anno Domini, 1740 and in the Fourteenth year of His majesties reign.*[39]

Seth knew that some of his father's remaining land, together with stock and household belongings, would eventually be signed away to each sister as she married. The core of the farm, however, belonged to him, with its orchard, garden, barn, sheds and pens all fanning out from a house that, despite its added kitchen, was beginning to show its age, especially the west end that grandfather Timothy had built in something of a hurry back in 1651.

For twenty years of marriage, Seth and Hannah put up with old-house inconvenience, likely knowing during the first decade that John wouldn't hear of wasting money on something as extravagant as fixing up what wasn't broken. The father died in 1751, but by then Hannah was managing two babies. She had already turned thirty when her first, Patty, was born. Timothy, named for the ancestor, came three years later and the littlest, Hannah, two and a half years after that. Between children underfoot and parents in their seventies, all needing tending, Mistress Dwight was likely the one who put a stop to any thought of construction during the second decade.

Aha! Moment: Hidden Treasure

Eventually things calmed down, in the way of families. Eighty-year-old Elizabeth Dwight seasonably followed her husband to the grave. The children were old enough to be out from underfoot. This would be a good time to address a whole range of old-house problems. The cross-gabled roofline and leaded-glass windows of Timothy Dwight's original section were hopelessly out of date, as were gaping fireboxes in the hall and parlor. The chimney itself wasn't any great shakes, and the original sills—the carrying beams that barely held the oldest part of the house off the ground—were rotting.

Imposing new houses had started to go up all around them, filling in the village center. Seth's brother-in-law, William Plimpton, had built brand-new when he married Kezia Dwight in 1725. In 1745, the new minister constructed a manse on North Street. Joshua Fisher had put up a grand building along the high road toward Dedham. Seth must have compared notes with builders over the years as he made do with what was his. What's in fashion these days? How do we elevate what we have to something bigger, better? Our family and our house both are the heart of the town. What's to be done to make the outward and visible sign a true reflection of those within—solid, wealthy, gracious, proud?

—You could just start over. Pick another spot on your five hundred acres and build from scratch.
No location as good as this. None so near our kinfolk, our neighbors. Our easy home fields.

—You could just add on to the east end and tear down the old part.
Ground gets iffy over there. Damp. Water underground from the rise behind us. The Lord knows our cellar's wet enough come spring.

—How about building off the back east end and still tearing down the west?
Nah. We'd be facing east, swamp nearly at our front door. We'd lose the south sun. We'd no longer face the common, the meetinghouse, the center of things. Nah. We'll keep the house just where it is, thank you. But tidied up. Bigger. A few new-fangled moldings and geegaws wouldn't hurt.

But how do you build a major addition while life needs to go on, in something like normal fashion, in the same house? Two centuries later, house historians spent days examining the results, theorizing about chopped-off beams and reused sleepers, unexpected steps and sealed-up wall openings. The explanation they came up with was not what we wanted to hear. In 1760 or so, they said, half the house had been torn down and replaced. Nothing we saw in 1998 was Timothy Dwight's original house. Did this mean we were wrong? Nothing had survived from the frontier building that withstood Indian attack? Had we lost our claim to "first and oldest"?

While we were stewing, and doubting the experts because they weren't telling us what we wanted to hear, preservation work began at the Dwight-Derby House. The project was massive. One part of it involved removing all the shingles from the lower walls, cutting out rotten sheathing boards to expose ant-ridden posts and crumbling sills and replacing the old framework with new oak beams to hold the house up for another hundred years.

One morning, I stopped by to see the progress and was met by an ecstatic crew. Architect, construction foreman and building crew were all beaming at a hole in the wall as if they had just found King Tut's tomb. "Come see what we found!" I did, and was, I thought, suitably impressed by a new oak beam neatly tucked under a cluster of old posts that were obviously worse for wear.

Three corner posts side by side near the front door are rare evidence of Timothy Dwight's house, John's and Seth's additions.

"Not that. Larry just realized there are three posts!" The significance of this still eluded me. They pointed more specifically to their treasure.

"This [pointing to the right-hand one] is the corner post you can see in the parlor [the old room with the lamb's tongue stops]. This [the left-hand one] is in the front hall. Which means this one in the middle [the one whose bottom end looked like a rotten tooth] is the corner post of Timothy's original house!"

Builders, from the seventeenth century on, had worked with what was already there, sistering new beams to old ones, letting the old carry some of the load. That way an earlier corner post could still hold the roof up while the addition was framing in—a colonial lally column of sorts.

The solution conceived by Seth Dwight and his builder was perhaps obvious but by no means simple of execution: Tear down the old part, Timothy's 1651 house. Save the nails, such as could be. Save the shutter hardware. Save the planed, smooth-surfaced floorboards and partition boards, the upper framing members that had stayed dry. Stand them up against the barn wall or stack them in a corner of the yard. Only the pieces too far gone get dragged away and—what? Fuel a raging bonfire in celebration of a new year, new house? Or just sit in a heap against a boundary wall, slowly sinking into compost over years to come?

Meanwhile, life proceeds in a somewhat normal fashion within the remaining east end and the kitchen. The rooms are crowded with too much furniture and noisy with hammering and the screech of crowbars levering boards off the frame. From time to time, the connecting wall by the chimney shakes. You take your life in your hands drawing water from the well out back if the men are working nearby.

Next, frame up a new west end to the size you want the whole to be: two stories high with a big attic and a sill raised off the ground, away from the damp and the bugs. Higher ceilings, too, by a good four or five inches, so the Dwight family (who run to tall men) can stop ducking their heads.

From a modern builder's perspective, a major problem emerges from all this raising of floors and ceilings on the new west end: the new floor levels no longer line up with the older, east end of the building. There is a six-inch differential between the new west parlor floor and the old east one, across the front of the house. The same is true upstairs, in the small hallway between the front bedrooms. The difference doesn't show up in the back part of the house because there, the 1690s shed roof over the kitchen was being replaced by a full second story with all new rooms.

It is likely that the eighteenth-century house carpenter did not see this height difference as a problem—he may even have done it on purpose, since he cared about structural stability, not handicapped access. As a result of the difference, the new horizontal framing pieces—the sills and plates—could be set right *on top of* the beams of the earlier building. Pin old and new together with good big trunnels and nothing was going to pull apart.

Rebuild the chimney then. It had already been changed once, when John added on the kitchen fifty years before. This time, the fireboxes in the new part were shrunk in size, with flaring walls that pushed more heat out to where it was needed. Hearths were raised to the new floor level in the front rooms and the kitchen, too. Here Elizabeth can be heard putting her foot down, overriding Seth's protests that the rear bake oven was dangerous and outmoded, declaring that the vast cooking fireplace had served well enough for two generations and needed no change—not so long as she was cook in the family.

The new house skeleton was almost complete. One last change required a spell of good weather and hard labor to accomplish. It was time for Elizabeth to move up the hill to sister Plimpton's house for the duration while Seth, with the nameless builder and his men, tore the roof off the east end of their own building. Cross-gabled rooflines had gone out of fashion with the seventeenth century.

A few days later, Elizabeth could stand at the Plimptons' back door and look downhill to a clean, straight ridgeline. It flanked the center chimney in pleasing symmetry, emphasizing the breadth of the house and almost—*almost*—tricking the eye into believing that the building's architectural elements were tidily balanced in good Georgian fashion.

They were not. The builders tried. They replaced the old front door with a handsome four-paneled one under a classic gabled pediment. They replaced small casement windows with big, double-hung, nine-over-six sash—even going so far as to saw up into the first-floor plate of the east end so that the new windows would line up with those in the west end. But when all was said and done, the east end of the house was still four feet wider than the west end, and its windows were clumped unevenly on each side of the door.

If the builders had only stretched their new frame by four feet, the house would have come out perfectly balanced, perfectly Georgian. Why didn't they? There is no reason to doubt their measurement capability. They must have known that they were building an imbalanced whole.

The only logical explanation for the four-foot shortfall lies in an unexpectedly modern decision: despite the teardown, they were retaining the original building "footprint"—the cellar, in other words, and a solid stone foundation wall that must have lain under Timothy Dwight's original house. Even Seth was not willing to foot the extra expense and labor of hand digging and reconstructing a cellar just to gain four feet that nobody would likely notice anyhow.

The almost-new house was finished "in a neat and workmanlike manner," as contracts of the period phrased it. In fact, the interior was more than neat. The new front parlor boasted fine wainscot paneling around three walls and a handsome fully paneled fireplace surround, complete with warm storage cupboards and stylish deep moldings. Granted, the panels weren't exactly matched in size on both sides of the fireplace. Maybe the builder had a pattern to follow that didn't quite fit the room. He had to work around an

West parlor paneling on the fireplace wall.

old-fashioned hearth, tucked in a corner, not centered like a proper Georgian firebox. But he shaved down the panel dimensions so that they would serve and covered the whole wall of this best room with neatly finished rectangles of light and shadow, high and low. Newly painted, the panels caught the western light from four big windows and must have glowed. If the sun proved too bright, the street outside too busy or the winter drafts too cold, handy interior shutters could be unfolded from deep window casings where they hung invisible, to be drawn across the small glass panes.

Other changes were made to simplify life for a younger-generation family whom Seth and Hannah could expect to move in when the children grew up. Two staircases led to the upper floor: the center front stair and a second off the kitchen that lined up with the east end rooms. On the west side of the house, a new door off the kitchen gave access to the barn, while a narrow doorway in the east parlor opened into the orchard. The new arrangements offered some privacy and a separation between generations.

The separation didn't reach as far as kitchen tasks. There was only one cooking hearth in the Dwight house, one stair or ladder down to the cellar with its casks, jars and bottles, one stairway up to the new attic where bags of dry goods lay and one direct route to the well. The kitchen was the only part of the Dwight house that did not substantially change during the great makeover. That would wait for another century and another woman's influence.

CHAPTER 2

Townsends

1745–1821

Neighbors

From 1745 until the end of the century, the Dwight family's story—and eventually their house—became inextricably linked with a newcomer to town. Jonathan Townsend entered Medfield history with a newly minted Harvard degree in 1745. He was invited to assist the Reverend Mr. Baxter in his duties, but the ailing pastor of the Medfield church died within months of Townsend's coming, and the young man "accepted the call" to succeed him. The town gave him a generous settlement to do so: £400 as the eighteenth-century equivalent of a signing bonus, plus an annual salary of £200; the right to farm town land adjacent to John and Seth Dwight's place; and a "pessel [parcel] of land" near the meetinghouse for him to build on.

A year and a half later, Townsend recorded in his journal: "1747, May 20. My Father with the family came to Medfield—a very pleasant day. My House was raised with much expedition without any hurt. We dined at three—things went on very safely, comfortably, regularly & decently."[40]

Seth and John Dwight were likely part of the house-raising crew—certainly observers—since, besides their own recent building experience, they were the new pastor's closest neighbors.[41] Townsend's house lot was just across North Street from the Dwights'.

Surprisingly, despite the minister's bachelor status and lack of family money, the building he put up would later be described as a "mansion house"—a term indicating size and solidity, if not necessarily elegance. Perhaps Townsend put his signing bonus into materials, erecting a structure designed to represent—to embody—the stature of one of Medfield's most influential public officials. The mansion house also had the capacity to shelter many children, an extended family and a variety of servants—all of which it would do over the next 125 years.[42]

A year and a half into Jonathan Townsend's ministry, with his house well finished and affairs in order, he brought Sarah Allen to Medfield as his bride. For forty years, the Townsend and Dwight families would support, commiserate with and console one another through a long string of personal tragedies, of which only shreds of evidence remain. No evidence at all remains of the normal times and family celebrations that must have offered some balance to tragedy.

Seth and Hannah Dwight were only five years older than the Reverend and Mistress Townsend. The Dwights had children first: Patty was born in 1747, followed by family namesake Timothy in 1750. Meanwhile, members of the older Dwight generation were getting on. Father John was seventy-six when he died, the same year the Townsends' first child came. The child died too. Two years later, Dwight and Townsend wives were both pregnant at the same time. Baby Hannah Dwight lived, but again a Townsend baby—a boy this time—died. In 1754, another Townsend baby was born, a girl named Sarah for her mother, and she survived.

Three healthy Dwight children in six years: the old Medfield family might expect to find itself with another houseful of children soon, as it had been during Seth's boyhood, when six of them had elbowed for space around the table. But surprisingly, Hannah Dwight bore no more children after her namesake. Things were quite different in the Townsend household.

Over the next nine years, Hannah Dwight saw Sarah Townsend through the births of five more children. Then, in 1761, Mrs. Townsend held Mrs. Dwight's hand and hugged young Sarah close as they wept over eight-year-old Hannah Dwight's death. Two years later, both the little Townsend boys died on one awful May day. No record identifies the causes of death, only their date. Did they succumb to one of the waves of smallpox that thinned the Commonwealth's population? Or perhaps was the disaster something as local as drowning in the millpond across the way? Even the mourning is implicit.

At the Townsends', a month-old baby was unaffected by the May tragedy: Horatio, whose paternal decision years later saved the Dwight-Derby House for posterity. And finally, the last Townsend child was born in the summer of

1766. Later in life at least, Gregory was blind and suffered from some nervous affliction. Had there been a complicated birth? Did the same complication lead to his mother's death six months later after only "a short illness in her husband's absence," as the family book states?[43] Sarah Townsend was only forty-four and might have been expected to live another thirty or forty years past childbearing. Whatever the cause, Jonathan Townsend returned from a December absence to a household of motherless children.

Sarah, the oldest, was twelve when she lost her mother, old enough to be stunned by the event and young enough to be weighed down by the domestic responsibility she inherited. There were the infant and three-year-old Horatio to tend. George and Mary were only six and five. Maybe Patty Dwight, grown up now, came to help out. Maybe, in exchange for Mr. Townsend's tutoring, Timothy Dwight was talked into chopping wood, showing off his sixteen-year-old manliness to any who would notice (as many young ladies did, some to their regret in later years). Neighbors supported neighbors in times of need.

Despite neighborly support, ongoing dissention within Pastor Townsend's congregation, perhaps mixed with the strain of early widowhood, pushed him to an extraordinary decision. By 1769, Townsend felt his position as leader of Medfield's flock had become untenable. The man who, in good Puritan form, was used to delivering sermons in two-hour increments wrote the briefest pronouncement of his career to his congregation: "Beloved—Sensible of my unworthiness of being continued in the relation of pastor unto you, I hereby request your dismission of me therefrom."

His request was granted. In the spring of the same year, he wrote his will, stating that everything he owned was to be equally divided among his children, each son to get his share when he turned twenty-one and each daughter when she turned eighteen or married. This was a traditional will, equally caring of each of his children. It was unusual only in the fact that Jonathan Townsend was just forty-eight, not an age at which most men would be contemplating eternity. As it turned out, his foresight would be needed in the coming decade.

* * * * * * *

In contrast to the Townsends' inward-looking household, by the 1770s the Dwight family patriarch, Seth, could see in Timothy, his only son, promise of the next step up the ladder of respectability. Seth continued to manage the four-hundred-acre estate, allowing Timothy to prepare for Harvard—

likely tutored by their friend and neighbor Jonathan Townsend. Timothy trained as a physician, and during the American Revolution he served as a surgeon's mate. By that time, however, Timothy had also sired a baby girl, whose mother was identified in town records only by her first name. He was claimed as father to at least one other child in town in the years that followed. A century later, the town historian would tersely comment, "He is said to have been a dissipated man."[44] Whatever Timothy Dwight's moral constitution, he clearly had no desire to spend the rest of his life in Medfield. After the war, he married a doctor's daughter who was sixteen years his junior and moved to Long Island, where he set up practice. His practice began, though, when smallpox came to Medfield.

The year 1776 has gone down in American history as the year of independence. Less well known is that 1776 was one of the smallpox epidemic years that recurred throughout colonial American history. Some may remember the story of future president John Adams volunteering to be inoculated with the new smallpox vaccine, signing himself into a Boston hospital to be infected and writing daily to Abigail as they both waited for the outcome of his dangerous, but ultimately successful, course of action.

From Boston to the smallest town, communities designated some site as a smallpox hospital, although for most towns and their residents, these were less places of healing than pesthouses where those who contracted the disease went into quarantine, and a few walked out again. Medfield had such a building, isolated from the rest of town on a small patch of land among the Noon Hill woodlots. Why father Seth Dwight was not taken to Noon Hill when he contracted smallpox in 1776 is unknown. One might guess that remaining in a comfortable home, tended by survivors of some earlier bout of the disease, would have to be infinitely preferable to conditions in an overcrowded, closed-up, run-down cottage.

According to the story, Jonathan Townsend sat with Seth Dwight in his last illness and prayed with him at his death in November. Then Townsend came down with the disease himself. Unlike Dwight, Townsend had a family of unexposed young people to protect. He sought out the best care available: the smallpox hospital in Dedham, where Dr. James Gerauld was doing his highly trained best with experimental vaccine to save those he could. Townsend was not one of them. On December 12, the Reverend Mr. Jonathan Townsend died, leaving behind in Medfield a family whose senior member was twenty-two-year-old Sarah.

* * * * * * *

The death of a father changes everything, and in this case personal loss was compounded by fear of the smallpox all around them in the winter of 1776. But all of this was also taking place at one of the most traumatic times in New England history: the British occupation of Boston, the closure of its port to shipping and the polarization of the colonies into two vehemently opposing camps. For the Dwight family, the political turmoil of the American Revolution turned personal loss into economic opportunity over the next two decades.

Mourning came first, by tradition. Just as Dorcas Dwight waited a year and a day after Timothy's death before she married John Adams in 1677, Patty Dwight was married 366 days after her father died, in 1777. Her new husband was no stranger. Jonathan Metcalf had grown up half a mile away, on Bridge Street. He had inherited the whole of his family's estate, which would have been a good start for a farmer's life, but Metcalf had other plans. He went into commerce instead, setting himself up as a "trader," apparently opening one of the newfangled dry goods stores that were just catching on after the Revolution—predecessors of the ubiquitous country store of the next century. This was a moment when a savvy trader could make a small fortune without undue effort, satisfying the long pent-up demand felt by every colonist for the most basic imported goods.

The challenge of commerce then, as now, was to come up with capital to pay for the stock in trade—the imported creamware dishes and fancy tea sets, bolts of calico and spools of lace, gentlemen's mourning rings and canes, shoe and knee buckles, tea and spices. One thing Metcalf could do was sell off parcels of his family land, which he did. Another way to acquire capital was to engage other investors in the plan, which he also did, in a roundabout way. He married Patty Dwight—mature, in her mid-thirties like himself, heir to half of her father's four-hundred-odd acres of prime agricultural land and sister of a man who had already made it clear that farming was not in his future.

The deal was sealed in October 1777, a month before the wedding. Timothy and Patty Dwight nominally "sold" their portion of the Dwight inheritance to Jonathan Metcalf for £450. In part, this may have been only a paper transaction, representing Patty's dower gift to Metcalf, who, on their marriage, would own all of her property to do with as he wished anyway. Some of the £450 may have been a cash payment to Timothy to outfit him for the army or pay support to the woman (or women) whose children he had sired.

Jonathan Metcalf moved into the Dwight house, and as in earlier generations, he and Patty shared it with mother-in-law Hannah. The Metcalfs had four children between 1778 and 1783. Jonathan's stature in the community rose to such an extent that he became a selectman in 1784—the same year that Tilden describes him as having been the "village storekeeper."[45]

Archaeological and architectural evidence at the Dwight-Derby House suggests that Metcalf may have run his store out of the southeast parlor—the old, seventeenth-century corner room that faced the town common and the millpond, within easy reach of Medfield's center crossroads. An exterior doorway had been cut through the wall in that room, while a large array of creamware ceramic shards (as well as hundreds of other artifacts) were embedded in the ground outside. Possibly, a lean-to was built outside the door, or perhaps a porch and steps for customers.

But more was going on inside the house than commerce. In 1786, Timothy Dwight sold off any remaining interest he may have had in his father's estate to his sister's husband Jonathan, apparently to keep himself out of trouble with the law. Meanwhile, mother Hannah wrote her will, pointedly dismissing her son Timothy with an inheritance of ten shillings "which together with what he has already had out of this Estate in Medfeild aforesaid I think his full share."[46]

Hannah had reason to be fed up with her son for more than his philandering. Timothy and Jonathan's investment plans had become embroiled in the same economic panic that led to Shays' Rebellion farther west in Massachusetts. For Metcalf and Dwight, the panic resulted in a number of creditors calling in debts at the same time. In more than a half-dozen lawsuits, the two were ordered to immediately pay over £376 in debts they had accrued. Outer fields and farmlands were sold piece by piece and still did not cover the debt. They were effectively bankrupt, and Jonathan—now the only legal property owner—sold the 150-year-old Dwight homestead to Marshall Spring, a Watertown physician.[47]

During the decade that followed Timothy married respectably and moved to Long Island. The Metcalf family moved to Boston, where they apparently continued in commerce, with Patty establishing herself as a milliner. By 1796, Marshall Spring finally owned the Dwight homestead free and clear, and he cashed in his investment by selling to Moses Hill, a local gentleman who died almost immediately. Gentleman or not, Hill's debts at his death totaled more than half the value of his entire estate, and the probate court ordered his administrator to sell the Dwight house to pay for them.

The administrator's curt record of what followed gives no hint of the decree's significance to future generations: "The Home Farm and Buildings sold to Horatio Townsend."[48]

Aha! Moment or Wild Goose Chase?

One day while I was poking through files in the Medfield Historical Society, I came across a reference to Derby family papers located at—of all unexpected places—West Point. The Derbys were related to the Townsends; the Townsends were connected to the Dwight house so, conceivably, the West Point papers might bear some passing relation to the story I was trying to reconstruct. Besides, doing research at West Point seemed like a glamorous idea. I packed my bag, said goodbye to family and house and drove off into the sunset. Closer to sunrise, really, but I was going west.

The trip from Medfield to West Point is only five hours, but for someone who dreads road trips and rarely goes anywhere without company, it was a major excursion. Three hours into the drive, I began wondering why this had seemed like a good idea. So what that the USMA archives had some sort of papers having to do with George Derby? Granted, Derby was born in Medfield, but his claims to fame were his career as a satirist (working out of San Francisco) and his association with the renowned West Point class of 1846; his classmates included Civil War greats like Ulysses S. Grant. I could look forward to reading obscure political commentary and maybe seeing his academy records. What kind of connection could I expect to make with small-town New England? Obviously, this was a wild goose chase. If I had any sense I would turn around and go home.

I didn't go home. Thoughts of scholarly due diligence kept me driving west; kept me in Highland Falls, New York, despite the sugar ants that lived under my run-down motel bed; kept me on target as I negotiated security checkpoints and finally walked into the high-ceilinged, book-filled space that is the United States Military Academy Archives. I was handed a checklist of holdings pertaining to George Horatio Derby and the first volley of Aha!s went off.

It had never occurred to me that the George Derby papers were actually Townsend-Derby family archives, donated to the Academy by a twentieth-century family member who believed West Point to be the unifying experience among generations of Derbys.[49] It had also never occurred to me that the family archives consisted of every scrap of paper and correspondence concerning George Derby from earliest childhood until his death, saved and treasured by an adoring mother. Boyish sketches—first copy work, then drawings of scenes outside his Medfield window. Homesick notes from the Boston school where he'd been placed to curb his wildness, and painful exchanges between mother and frustrated schoolmasters who could not mold the youth to expectations. Mary Derby's determined campaign to win George a nomination to West Point and the evolution of boy to man at the academy, where he discovered a use for his offbeat talents.

There were eleven acid-free archival boxes and an oversized folio of George's drawings. Nineteenth-century Medfield was there. The Dwight-Derby House was there. The Townsend-Derby family emerged from history's shadows to literally and figuratively replace the Dwights as central characters in the house on Frairy Street.

A NEW ORDER

During the same two decades that Timothy Dwight and Jonathan Metcalf were brashly testing the economic waters of independent America, the Townsends were facing a very different struggle. The confrontation had been coming for over a decade. Medfield, like most of the farm towns surrounding Boston, abhorred the Stamp Acts and what were seen as growing British infringements on colonial civil rights. In cities like Boston, however, opinion was not so cut and dried. Boston was a commercial and administrative center; its inhabitants depended for their livelihoods on the colony's interactions with Great Britain. So when, following the Boston Tea Party in 1773, the colonists first declared an embargo on British imports and, subsequently, the English Board of Trade closed the port of Boston to all shipping, the line became clear between those who did and those who did not place the economic interests of the empire above the political rights of colonial citizens.

Many of the families affected by this polarization—like the Boston Hutchinsons, the Royalls of Medford and the Brownes of Salem—had long been international investors and saw no real decision to be made: they were Loyalists to the end, horrified that British citizens should rise up against their own government and the economic system that underwrote their entire way of life. In the course of the war to come, whole families left the country, returning to England or establishing new lives for themselves as exiles across the Canadian border.

For other families, like the Townsends and their kin, allegiance was much more complicated, influenced by diverse occupations, residences and family history. Medfield's Townsend family was closely tied to the Needham Townsends through brother Samuel, a successful merchant. They were equally closely tied to brother Gregory Townsend, a Boston merchant. It would appear that Samuel Townsend supported the Patriot cause. The Reverend Jonathan Townsend had been silent on the subject. But Gregory Townsend was a Loyalist, a firm supporter of the British government. He was also a supplier to the royal troops that occupied Boston between 1776 and March 1777.

Did the Patriot troops that barricaded the city allow Gregory to pass through the lines to attend his brother's funeral in December? Was he permitted to send money to his brother's family, left without income at Jonathan's death? The questions are almost moot, for in 1778 Gregory Townsend was proscribed—banished from Massachusetts for consorting with the enemy. He moved to New York, becoming assistant commissary general to the British army. At the end of the war, he emigrated to the new settlement of Halifax, Nova Scotia, to join hundreds of other Loyalist refugees.[50] Over the next twenty years, Gregory rebuilt his life and a respectable fortune. In the interim, almost all of his property was confiscated by the new Massachusetts government, so his brother's Medfield family felt his loss twice over.[51]

Gregory Townsend had taken his familial responsibility to heart, however, carefully leaving a letter of credit with Mary and Daniel Hubbard, relatives by marriage whose political sympathies, if not visibly patriotic, were at least muted enough to allow them to remain in New England.[52] Over the decade that followed, brother Samuel helped out as well, and there are letters among family members staying with Samuel in Needham, or visiting the Hubbards in Newport, Rhode Island, in a sort of familial musical chairs that shifted with the seasons. One letter, written by Sarah Townsend in 1782, updated the young Townsends' progress. It was a carefully thought-out letter, polite and respectful, never referring outright to Gregory's Loyalist politics, Uncle Samuel's disinterest, her own loneliness or her lack of marital expectations. Addressed to New York, the letter was written "to my ever dear and honor'd Uncle":

> *As you have been so kindly interested in the happiness of your friends here, I with pleasure inform you that all our connections are well…*
>
> *My Uncle Samuel's family appeared were well just before I left home, but we see very little of him, his own cares take up too much of his attention, to leave much room for us…*
>
> *My brothers are scattered about in the wide world. Jon[a]. is in this place, ingag'd in the writing way. George at Mendon carrying on his business there. Horatio has entered his last year at Coledg. Your namesake Gregory is a prentice to a Sadler, a business he chose. I could have wish'd him, if it was*

> *only for the sake of his name to have moved in a higher sphere, but he poor child, by reason of deafness, made but little improvement of those advantages he was favor'd with, while under the eye of a tender parent, and after that, his Situation was by no means calculated to improve his mind, or inlarge his capacities. Polly and I as yet continue in the place of our nativity.*[53]

Horatio's "Coledg" was Harvard, which the Townsends' many connections and his Uncle Gregory's money made it possible for him to attend.

By 1784, Horatio Townsend was an up-and-coming young lawyer, perhaps practicing in Medfield or in the larger town of Dedham. He lived in the family home with Sarah, Mary (nicknamed "Polly") and their brother Gregory, the saddler. Across the millpond, widow Hannah Dwight, daughter Patty Metcalf and her husband were still living in the old Dwight homestead. And somewhere nearby was a country place owned by Nathaniel Greene, a Boston merchant with a city home on Newbury Street. The Greenes, like many prosperous city dwellers, maintained a rural farm to provide both fresh food for the household and fresh air for the family during warm months of the year. A wistful note from their son Thomas, traveling on business in Charleston, echoes the farm's essential role in family life: "P.S. A little of our Country produce would be very acceptable such as Potatoes, Beets & Turnips the latter of which are not to be had."[54]

Over the next decade, the lives of these two families would change considerably and become increasingly entwined. Horatio was accepted by the Greenes as a suitable escort for their daughter Anstis. In one letter her father writes that "if you please you can come home with him" from visiting with a friend. Two years later, it was Horatio who drove her to the Greenes' Boston home after the death of her sister. In 1787, the following year, it must have been Anstis's turn to support Horatio, for both his sister Mary and brother George died within months of each other, apparently from tuberculosis.

Not all was sickness and death. September 1795 found Horatio escorting Anstis back from Newport again. They were old friends by then, having known each other for over a decade. Surprisingly, at least for Anstis, both were in their mid-thirties and still unmarried. But one important factor had changed. Horatio Townsend was on the right side of local politics and about to become clerk of courts for the newly established Norfolk County. His incipient step up the social and economic ladder must have tipped the scales, for six months later, Horatio and Anstis married, and nine months after that Mary Townsend was born, the first of their five children within five years.

The young Townsend family was not permanently ensconced on North Street. When court was in session, the couple rented a house in Dedham, right next to the elegant new granite courthouse. Winter and spring were Dedham's busy seasons. The town was filled with lawyers and petitioners, judges and defendants taking part in the judicial system. Every available room and house were rented; stagecoaches along the great roads from Boston to Worcester, Hartford and New York delivered visitors to the town's coaching inns; shops and mills had more demand for goods than could be accommodated. The town had its own newspaper, the *Norfolk Advertiser*, which once a week delivered a four-page spread of news and commentary of world events, legal notices and local advertising. Lectures, debates, socials and dinners entertained the seasonal residents, whose influx set off a building boom unlike any the county had ever seen. Dedham's population tripled in the decade that followed its promotion to shire town for Norfolk County.

Come the heat of summer, however, or winter's ice and snow, Dedham largely returned to the sleepy, slow-paced country town it had been in 1790—or even 1690. And the Townsend family returned to Medfield, where they decided it was time to do something about their living situation. It had been fine for a bachelor to share a family home with unmarried siblings but it was less acceptable after marriage, and the arrival of a baby discombobulated the entire household. Sarah Townsend, Horatio's dowager sister, was less than enthusiastic about the infant. "The little one is very well and quiet," Sarah reported to her aunt Hubbard. "I cant say it is of much consequence to me at present, but dare say it will be if it lives."[55]

Family connections came to the rescue once again. The old social network between Townsends and the Dwight family, dating back over fifty years, had never lapsed. Even though the Dwight family's last interest in the old Frairy Street house had ended with widow Hannah's death in 1792, Sarah Townsend maintained her friendship with Hannah's daughter and granddaughter, both named Patty Metcalf, visiting back and forth and corresponding regularly with them. Metcalfs visited Townsends in Medfield, while Sarah wrote regularly to Patty and commissioned her to make caps and other items at her milliner's shop in Boston.

* * * * * * *

At the same time, though in a very different sphere, Medfield lawyer Horatio Townsend was privy to every probate judgment handed down by the bench in Norfolk County. Horatio was one of the first to note that the old Dwight house was going up for auction "at public vendue" to settle Deacon Hill's estate in Medfield, and he made sure that he was high bidder for the property: "The Home Farm and Buildings sold to Horatio Townsend $1640 sold May 9, 1797."[56] We are left to wonder if he may have been the only bidder.

That summer, he and Anstis moved their belongings across the small common from his father's house to the Dwight place. Their new home backed up on sixteen acres of land. There were barns and an old orchard, a small cider mill and a "small piece of Land nearby improv'd as a Garden." A functioning millpond spread before them, and the neighborhood was noisy during the week.

The new Townsend house—the old Dwight place—sat on the edge of Medfield's small village center. In 1797, the center bore little resemblance to the cluster of respectable houses, idyllic park and small shops that would come to characterize it in later years. Approaching town from Dedham and the east, a handful of solid Georgian homes stood on large lots—like the Townsend family house they were leaving—but as the roadway fanned out to a dirt common beside the meetinghouse, the character of its buildings became mixed. The meetinghouse, Medfield's civic and religious heart, was surrounded by a core of manufacturing and commercial establishments, many of them operating out of older homes, like the shop that Jonathan Metcalf had set up in the Dwight house.

Whether the Metcalf shop was still in operation when Horatio and Anstis bought the property is unknown, but certainly there were other shops around them, including Artemas Woodward's, located near the meetinghouse. To the west, a fenced pasture where John Frairy's house once stood served as a buffer between the house and the noise and bustle of a blacksmith shop at the dam. The small road that cut from North Street in front of their house—just a track, really—only led as far as swampy lowland a few hundred yards downstream. There, some enterprising Medfielder had set up a potash works, leaching chemicals out of the town's fireplace ashes to make lye for soap.

There is little evidence that the young Townsends changed their old house significantly. In fact, there would have been little time or money to be spent on home improvements, between Horatio clerking; Anstis dealing with five babies in five years and tending to her ailing mother in Boston; settling Uncle Gregory's estate in Halifax; and, eventually, overseeing elegant renovations to a city house of their own in Dedham.

In the meantime, there were visits back and forth to Boston and family to entertain and assist. Horatio's sister Sarah and brother Gregory continued to live in the family home across the pond, and Sarah became more and more ensconced in the role of maiden aunt and family nursemaid, traditional roles that she had been forced to adopt when her father died twenty years earlier. Sarah—or Aunt Sally, as the younger generation called her—was a regular correspondent who carefully saved drafts of her letters, building an archive that offers glimpses of the first Townsend generation to occupy the house on Frairy Street.

In 1799, this maiden aunt wrote to her sister-in-law about the birth of Horatio Jr.: "You have I presume, heard of the birth of the son the 28th… which has occasion'd great joy to all interested. My brother and sister highly delighted, Mary & Lucretia transported with their little Brother, and Aunt Sally rationally pleased."

Apparently, young Mary Townsend was a frequent visitor at her aunt's, and she had won Sarah's heart over baby sister Sarah, Aunt Sally's namesake. "I have got my Bro['s] little Mary with me, which serves a plaything for us, and saves Gregory getting quite out of spirits, she is very dear, and interesting to us, and for myself, I must own I love her with a too fond partiality, and don't know as my namesake will ever be of so much consequence to me, though she is a charming child now."

Patty Metcalf, daughter of Sarah's old Medfield friend and neighbor, was a regular visitor. More than once, Patty wrote thank-you notes from Boston, and country/city contrasts are clear in her words: "After enjoying the lovely, peacefull scenes that Medfield affords, & the pleasure of your society, I could not (I must confess) set down with so good a relish to my business amidst dust, smoke & hurry, & all the etcetera of a Milliners shop." Following another visit, Patty wrote:

> *My visits to M*[edfield], *I often recur to for entertainment, & they afford it of the most delightfull kind serene & placid, as the scene itself; your Pond is in imagination before me. I see it as from your house in a fine evening after sunset, when the Horizon is beautifully reflected in its clear bosom; I now listen at the chamber window & hear the murmuring of the brook, while the stillness that reigns around soothes my mind to tranquillity.*

The tranquility of Medfield was not enough to sustain Patty Metcalf. She died at the age of thirty-four. Her passing is noted in the Townsend papers with a carefully transcribed obituary, of which Sarah was likely the author. "Her piety, which governed her actions…; her cultivated mind which sought refuge…in reading and reflection; her industry that made her place reliance on herself; her amiable and affectionate disposition…; and her example of patient suffering and pious resignation, will not lose their reward."

Sarah was not totally isolated, as she kept house in Medfield and saw to her brother Gregory's failing health. An 1804 letter informs her that her broken silver teapot spout had been located in Boston: "found it had been made & waiting for some months Mr. Revere not knowing where to send it"—an unexpected glimpse of Paul Revere, the silversmith, and his country clientele.

In another 1804 letter, Sarah's polite expression of thanks masks the fact that she had managed to broker publication of a literary landmark. Writing to Mary Hubbard, her uncle Gregory's sister-in-law, she reported:

> *I have discharged the trust committed to me, for my friend Miss Adams, I wish you could have been witness of the emotion with which she received it. I shall not attempt to describe, but must beg you to let her generous Patron know, that his bounty is bestowed on one, whose modesty makes no claims, and whose…grateful sensibility upon this occasion has no bounds. be so good as to make my respects acceptable to Mr. H with thanks for the pleasure he has given, in making me the medium of communication.*[57]

Reading through the ornate language, it would appear that Daniel Hubbard sponsored the publication of Hannah Adams's *The Truth and Excellence of Christian Religion*, which came out in 1804. Adams, Medfield-born, was one of America's first female authors, categorized today as "the first woman in the United States who made literature a profession."[58] Her books on religious history were highly respected and her reputation as a literary light earned her a pension underwritten by some of Boston's leading citizens. Sarah Townsend was her literary agent.

It is not surprising that in later years, Mary Townsend Derby developed a reputation for intelligence and wit. She had learned at her aunt's knee.

* * * * * * *

While life proceeded at a slow pace in Medfield, the Townsend girls were growing up in Dedham. Mary, the eldest, was sixteen when a young man presented himself to her father with a letter of introduction:

Salem, March 30th 1813
Dear Sir—

Permit me to request your civilities and attention to the Bearer of this letter;—Mr. John B Derby, nephew of Mrs. Pickman—He is about to become a resident in Dedham for the purpose of reading law in Mr Richardson's Office—He is a young man of uncommon talents, and considerable acquirements, and as I believe of a good temper and disposition, but being of a social turn, and having a great taste for music, he has been rather volatile. He has a fondness for good company especially that of the Ladies, a circumstance which I consider much in his favor and a great security against his falling into low dissipation—The esteem and regard which I entertain for his Father, and the interest which I feel in his welfare—induce me to request you to keep a friendly eye over him and to introduce him to the respectable society of your Town—

yours with great esteem,
B Pickman jr.

John Barton Derby came well recommended and well blooded to the young and aspiring county town of Dedham. He was charming, a fine conversationalist, and promised to go far in the circles of legal power and social influence that governed Massachusetts. Horatio Townsend did as requested, opening his house and undoubtedly other, professional doors to Mr. Derby as well.

In the years that followed, John Derby could be found of an evening socializing with the younger Townsends, spending time as an older brother might with their only son, Horatio, and escorting and flirting with daughters Mary, Lucretia and little Sarah. He appears to have been an exemplar for Horatio Jr., who was less than enthusiastic about following in his father's footsteps at Harvard.

Derby had much to recommend him. "A young and brilliant lawyer… of an old and aristocratic Salem family[,] a man of elegant person and fascinating manners," one acquaintance remembered in later years, and echoed Pickman's observation that John Derby was "especially attractive to the female sex." One of Derby's college professors was more restrained. "He was distinguished in early life by his sprightliness and humor. He lacked only an elevated aim and steady purpose."[59]

Unfortunately, John Derby's "fondness for…the Ladies" tended to interfere with his advancement in business and society. In 1816, he married a seventeen-year-old clergyman's daughter from Northampton. Within a year, his young wife was dead. This episode in bare outline, evidenced only by vital records

Photo of pastel portrait identified as John Barton Derby. Location of original drawing unknown. *USMA Archives, George Derby Papers.*

of the towns involved, gives little hint of the uproar that must have accompanied it. John's father did continue limited financial support of his son, paying for the couple's board at John Guild's house in Dedham,[60] but all agreed that the bride was too young and her family was not on a par with the influential Salem Derbys. Hannah Barrell Derby's premature death brought suffering to family and husband alike, and the circumstances surrounding it would haunt him in later years. The brief dramatic episode hinted—to those who would listen—at John Derby's fatal character flaws: impulsiveness and a will to ignore any authority not conforming to his own desires. These tendencies would become driving forces in later years, pushing Derby into a maelstrom of vituperation and violence that sucked the Townsend family in with him.

AHA! MOMENT: THE HOARDER

Some weeks after my trip to West Point, when the information was shared and digested and the euphoria had worn off, I realized that even the Derby Papers had not answered all the questions. Big holes still remained in the story of the Frairy Street house and life in it. Biggest of all was the gap between a successful Townsend family in Dedham and Mary Townsend Derby's struggling Medfield sisterhood. That gap had to be filled to understand the house on Frairy Street and the company of women who lived in it for sixty years.

Then I remembered a strange letter I had copied from the USMA Archives: "Dear Mr. Riley, On October 27th I sent to you by Certified mail a package of old letters…I am planning to send one more box. This will contain miscellaneous documents." The letter, dated 1976, was addressed to the director of the Massachusetts Historical Society in Boston. The list was obscure but tantalizing, including "a folder of letters to & from Townsend-Metcalf; letter to his brother from Gregory Townsend and an extract from my Great Grandfather's almanac Dec. 1697 until 1783."

The MHS online catalogue, blessed with its ultimate bluestocking name "Abigail," is wonderfully efficient. There, under "Townsend Family Papers," I discovered the items described in the West Point letter, donated by Virginia Barton Derby of Florida. The catalogue description sent me racing to Boston: "Papers of the Townsend family of Medfield, Mass. The majority of the papers consists of letters among family members [including] Horatio's children, Mary, Lucretia, Horatio, and Sarah."

What I expected was so much less than what I found. Yes, the genealogy was there. One folder at the society was a documentary miscellany written over two hundred years that provided the "prequel" to the Derby saga. Pages written in scripts from different eras, signed by Townsends and Greenes, Hubbards and Allens—all related in one way or another—profiled ongoing parallel bloodlines of successful merchants and distinguished clerics. I finally made sense of the names that peppered public documents and the West Point papers. In fact, there was enough to paint a large biographical family portrait.

But the second folder contained something much rarer: an extraordinary collection of scribbled drafts and final letters by nineteenth-century Townsend family members. Everyday notes—the equivalent of phone calls—of visits and requests between Medfield and Dedham. Letters from Horatio, a horrified father eventually forgiving a daughter's waywardness. Letters between Mary Townsend—soon Mary Derby—and her family sketching a newlywed life that started badly and ended worse, as she struggled to make a home in Medfield as her husband devolved from adoring to abusive.

Letters like this are as rare as old work clothes. Almost inevitably, the next generation cleans house of these scraps of everyday life, throwing out whole layers of history with the trash. But the Townsends were different, starting with a youthful agreement between Mary and her favorite sister and correspondent, Sarah:

> *Notwithstanding my dread of* [an] *appearance some forty or fifty years hence in a book entitled "memoirs of Miss Sarah Townsend with selections from her diary and various correspondents" I am constrain'd in hopes of turning…your writing powers toward me, to write at this present…but when I reflect that the book will not probably be "put out" in my life time*

> *I am a little comforted especially as I think the letters cannot all be printed as* [they] *will swell the volume to too large a size*—[61]

Sarah was the hoarder who carefully saved the early Townsend-Derby correspondence. In time, it would find its way to the attic on Frairy Street, to a closet in Florida and, eventually, to a Boston archive, where it would reveal a close-knit society of Townsend women who visited, tended, encouraged and wrote to one another in an intergenerational network of mutual support.

In their letters, notes and jottings, I had discovered an ordinary family in extraordinary times, and over a hundred years of small-town America came to life in intimate detail. Often the documents spoke for themselves, their voices so clear that they needed no amplification.

CHAPTER 3
Derbys
1821–1880

STAR CROSSED

By 1819, John Derby had returned from mourning to his earlier socializing at the Townsend house in Dedham. Horatio Jr., meanwhile, found himself suspended from Harvard College, on the verge of flunking. Like many young men in similar situations, Horatio was sent out to the country to escape city distractions, and set to studying as a private pupil of a minister in nearby Sudbury. Older and wiser sister Mary sat down one July evening to cheer him up with a teasing letter: "Mother and Aunt Lucretia send a great deal of love to you, unworthy as you are. O! by the way, some people think you resemble me, do bear that in mind, and appear to the best advantage, that the comparison may not bring disgrace."

When her brief store of news had been exhausted she ended: "P.S. This page is to be fill'd by a hand more able," and a bolder handwriting begins:

> *Dear Doctor, The fountain of your amiable sisters ideas having dried up, she called on me to keep up the current of correspondence…I have no doubt that while in Cambridge you saw the fiend indolence acquiring daily more power over you, and made many resolutions to break his chains…Never despair, but look forward to an honorable station in your class & and honorable profession in life.*

The Townsend-Derby Family N

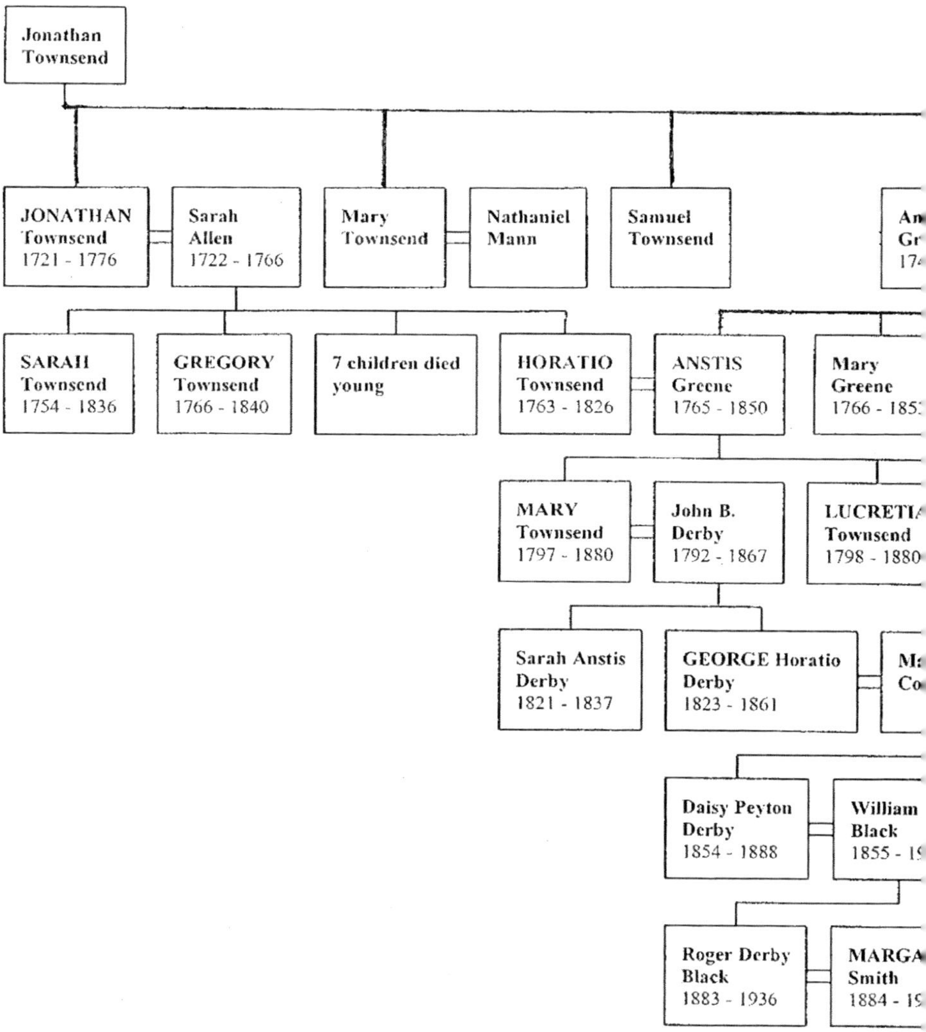

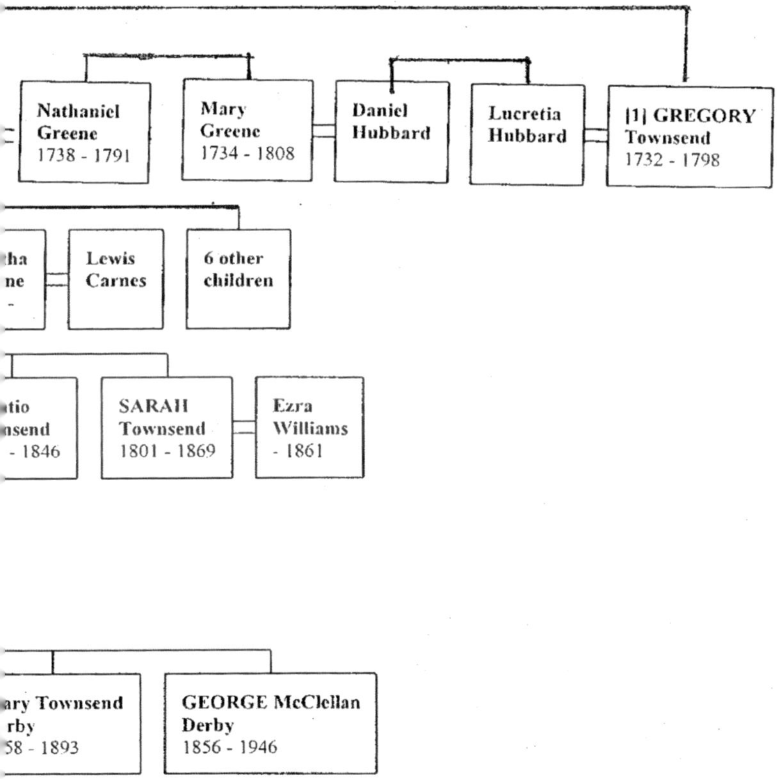
Nathaniel Greene 1738 - 1791
Mary Greene 1734 - 1808
Daniel Hubbard
Lucretia Hubbard
[1] GREGORY Townsend 1732 - 1798
tha
ne
Lewis Carnes
6 other children
tio
nsend
- 1846
SARAH Townsend 1801 - 1869
Ezra Williams - 1861
ary Townsend
rby
58 - 1893
GEORGE McClellan Derby 1856 - 1946

Bringing the letter to a close, the new correspondent, referring to Mary Townsend as "The perfection of Nature," comments, "we should like to look in upon your hermitship," and closes, "Excuse my freedom & ever believe me interested in your success and happiness—Yours & c.—J B Derby."[62]

This intimate scene—Mary and John, nominally chaperoned by her mother, bent over a letter together sharing laughter and concern—was repeated frequently in the year that followed, supplemented by carriage rides to visit Horatio, Sunday evening outings to a theatre newly opened in Dedham and whispered conferences perhaps not overheard, but definitely seen.[63]

In midwinter, Mary traveled the seven miles to Medfield for a stay with her sister Sarah and aunt Sally Townsend. Sarah (called "Amy" by her family to keep relationships straight) was installed in her aunt's house as a live-in companion. This common practice provided both suitable training for a teenage girl and necessary assistance for aging or ailing relatives. Throughout the Townsend correspondence, extended companion stays were frequent occurrences, and generations of Townsends, Hubbards, Greenes and Derbys shifted back and forth between Medfield, Dedham and Boston.

Mary's February visit was different, likely motivated by a parental wish to provide time for reflection and distance between her and Mr. Derby. What inspired such parental caution? Were there echoes of Mr. Pickman's long-ago introduction of the young man who showed a "fondness for good company especially that of the Ladies"? Did he continue to show a temperament that was "rather volatile"? Did his family's status among Salem's wealthiest merchants make him a socially inappropriate match for a respectable but small-town lawyer's daughter? Whatever the considerations, Mary's retreat to backwater Medfield was intended to revise her attitude concerning Mr. Derby—and it did so, though not as her parents might have wished. On her return to Dedham, Mary wrote a note to Amy, reflecting on her new-found maturity: "I miss the stillness and quiet comfort of aunt's little parlour. I do believe stillness and solitude is very congenial to my feelings, for all people think I am rather the reverse of sedate, though I know now I am as sober, and steady in my feelings, as anyone need be, whatever may have been the case."[64]

Sedate, sober and steady as she may have felt, Mary Townsend was still the object of John Derby's affections, as he was of hers. Horatio and Anstis Townsend were not the only parents to object to the liaison. By July, the situation had come to a head, and Horatio sat down to draft a letter to John Derby, the suitor's father. Using a single piece of paper, he added successive notes to the draft, the handwriting of each less controlled than the former one had been.

Dedham July 27th 1820

Dear Sir—I have just taken from the Post Office your [letter] *of the 26th…The connection you protest against is as much deprecated by me and all my family as it can possibly be by your self…—Your determination respecting your son, in the event of his marriage, is contrary neither to my expectation nor my wishes…*

To prevent a union so unpromising has been with me a single object, for a twelvemonth or in other words, from the time I first entertained a suspicion that it was contemplated.—I could say much more [but would prefer to do so in a confidential interview.] In the meantime permit me to say, that were your son perfectly independent of you in point of property, without your approbation I should never consent to the connection…

The marriage union should be a bond of union between two families,— And I would never receive as a son in law, your son or any man, who could not introduce his wife as a welcome daughter to his own parents—

Horatio's second note was more defensive: "My daughter will be always dear to me, and will be cherished and comforted as far as circumstances will afford of it, under every disaster, whether her misfortunes are the effect of her own indiscretions or are merely adventitious." And finally, distraught: "The information you received in the street is true, but it is too mortifying a truth for me to dwell upon."[65]

Amy Townsend's family register includes her permanent record of the cause of her father's distress, as well as a disturbing footnote:

August 6th 1820 Sunday P.M.
Mary Townsend was married to John B. Derby by Rev. Mr. Felch. they went to Medfield to live.
Nov 1822 Mother & Child returned to live at her Father's in Dedham.[66]

It wasn't as if Mary hadn't been warned. Whatever qualms the rest of her family voiced to her in the days between posting the banns and wedding John, Uncle Nathaniel Greene committed his fears to paper in a close-written four-page letter: "Never my dear Mary since the power of using the pen was given me did I take one with such painful such heart rending feelings, as I now do to write you."

Uncle Nathaniel must have been one of the Townsend family's last hopes to prevent the dreaded match between Mary and John. A prosperous Boston merchant, Greene knew and was trusted by the merchant families of Salem as well as Boston. He had just encountered John's uncle, Richard Derby, he reported, and then repeated word for word the outraged comments he had heard: "[Derby] askd if the young lady that Mr D was engagd to was any relation of [ours.] he said is the Parents willing; we told him not;…he said does she know his Character? does she know what a husband he made to his first Wife?"

But Uncle Nathaniel, knowing that the older generation's disapproval would not be enough to stop Mary, committed to paper other information current on the street—common knowledge, he indicated—concerning John's treatment of his first wife, the lovely young Hannah who died within a year of marriage: "The Gentleman who married his first wife's sister, said he pitied the young Lady [Mary Townsend] she did not know what she was to suffer, no doubt he would horsewhip her in three or four weeks after marriage. Others say he will be the means of your death by accident."[67]

Mary must have dismissed it all as hearsay, confident that her love and her husband's reassurances would make theirs a perfect union. She certainly refused to acknowledge Uncle Nathaniel's final insistent question: "Are you willing to be miserable the rest of your life, for a few weeks of what you may anticipate as pure felicity with the being you love?"

* * * * * * *

The twenty-seven months of Mary and John Derby's marriage defined the next era of life for the old farmhouse on Frairy Street. Some of what happened can only be guessed at. Some was documented by the inveterate letter writers and preserved by Sarah, the hoarder. In the long run, the survival of the house itself stood as testament to its owner's love and persistence.

The extent of Derby family disapproval was plain. John Barton Derby was disowned. This left the new husband with only a young lawyer's income for support of his new wife—a situation he had never had to deal with before. John made an effort to come up with funding. Within the month, he sold a small investment property in Dedham for $330, but it was clear that this would not go far.

Fortunately for the newlyweds, Horatio Townsend took a different approach, adhering to his earlier pledge to comfort his daughter as circumstances would afford. During the first year of their marriage, he allowed the couple to live in the Frairy Street house but made it clear that he did not wish to communicate with either of them. Mary kept up contact through letters to Amy, and her words echo the loneliness of banishment from family and Dedham society:

> *Wednesday evening December 27th 1820*
> *My dear Amy*
> *As I do not feel much inclin'd for work I think I will accept your invitation to keep a letter begun and finish it when I can…I have thought much of father and wish anxiously to hear from him…I presume you are over at Jeremy's looking desprit handsome and having a desprit smart time. I should have admired to go had they had the manners to send for us last week instead of this when they knew we were coming home. I assure you J* [John Barton] *did not feel much flatter'd.*[68]

Living conditions in Medfield were less than optimal, although Mary presented it in the best light possible. The writing on her next letter to Amy was brown. "[January 9, 1821]…my poor unlucky ink has froze all the black out of its once ebony complexion…you do not know how snug huz and I look here wish you could just pop your head in and see—the curtains all drawn he reading and I working or writing to you or reading if I chuse to."[69]

By February, Horatio Townsend softened his stance toward his daughter. He was suffering from increasingly painful bouts of a progressive illness that would drag on for four more years. Adding to this worry, Mary was pregnant. Horatio was driven to make more permanent arrangements for her protection and long-term support while he was still able.

Financial support for a woman in the early nineteenth century normally came from one of two sources: her male blood relatives if she was single or her husband if she was married. Marriage introduced a complicating factor, since any real estate owned by the wife was legally considered to be the husband's property, to dispose of as he wished. That was the last thing Horatio wanted to see happen, so he put his legal training to work. In the spring of 1821, he signed a bond stating that while Mary would normally expect to receive $1,200 from his estate after his death, if he allowed her "to take immediate possession of and quietly occupy and improve a certain house lot and the house and barn thereon standing lying in Medfield," then the debt would be considered paid.[70] The bond did not give Mary ownership of the house—only the right to occupy it—and thus John Derby would not have the right to sell it out from under her. Whatever Derby thought of the arrangement, he conveyed the news from Dedham to Medfield, and Mary was quick to write her father a long, solicitous and loving letter that included her thanks.

> *I thank you my dear father for the kind offer you made me through Mr Derby. I hardly know how to express my gratitude for generosity I have so ill deserv'd…I hope Mr Derby will not find the repairs too expensive, or will receive assistance from his father, which will enable us to accept your bounty and welcome you (to see how prettily we shall be fix'd there)…M^r^ D said you would come this week if the weather was good, and look into affairs a little, and I hope you will, and bring Mother with you if you can conveniently, as we are quite zealous to begin gardening, and already in imagination see great improvements, and have appropriated one chamber to the girls.*[71]

A month later, Mary and John went to Boston in a vain search for financial assistance. Mary's mother commented on the outcome: "I am not surprised that Mr. Ds Father—will not meet you in Boston; and if I may be allowed to give my oppinion about it—think it would be better for Mr. Derby to go to Salem, and see his Father as he told me he would."[72]

Despite setbacks on the Derby side, the Medfield house began to see improvements. "Our home is going on by degrees," Mary wrote. "I feel very anxious to get fix'd there as soon as possible it looks very pleasant and everyone begins to say 'what a delightful place you have got Mr Derby' it has grown healthy and delightful all of a sudden," despite the fact that she christened the house "frog hall"—adding, "why is not that a very good name?"[73]

As the summer and Mary's pregnancy progressed, she began to feel the confinement that accompanied motherhood. John Derby seemed overly solicitous, and Mary wrote a frustrated note that she insisted he deliver to her siblings in Dedham: "I have anticipated the pleasure of seeing you this week and should go with Mr Derby today but the weather is such that he thinks it not proper or prudent for me…I want to go today most horribly."

On October 19, 1821, Sarah Anstis Derby was born in Dedham, where Mary's family could take care of mother and child. Over the months that followed, there was visiting back and forth from Dedham to Medfield; Sarah Anstis survived apparent bouts of colic; John Derby first moved his household into the upper chambers of the house for warmth and then insisted that the bedroom be moved downstairs because "Mr D finds we burn too much wood." Derby was also appointed justice of the peace, undoubtedly improving his income, but also requiring more of his time in Dedham, away from his young family.

Mary was not always alone. A girl came in to help with household chores, and both Mary's mother and sisters came visiting. Other days, she would carry the baby up the street to Aunt Sally's house or to look in on Uncle Gregory, who made an early impression on Sarah, as Mary reported to Amy: "My dear little babe has just waked up and is talking very pretty in her cradle. she is very interesting and sensible and says Uncle Gregory very plain. I hope she will say grand pa next." Yet until spring, life for Mary and the baby was circumscribed by the cold, despite her protests to the contrary. "Our room is so warm and comfortable that we don't feel the cold at all and I don't know when it is cold unless someone tells me."[74]

April brought welcome change. Toddler Sarah was delivered to Dedham for a grandparents visit, while Amy rode out to Medfield for a stay with Mary. Their days may have been taken up with spring cleaning, but the chance for two best friends to spend time together—without the distraction of child or husband either, as court was likely in session—must have been a welcome relief after the winter's isolation. Mary Derby was young and outgoing. She was used to the round of events and activities that characterized Dedham's more lively milieu and being with the close-knit family she adored. She had not yet made a place for herself in Medfield's small-town society and was in fact preparing to be confirmed in Dedham's Episcopal church.

Even the house she occupied stood on the edge of respectability—across the millpond from a window and shutter manufactory, next door to a blacksmith, in a neighborhood of artisans, boarders and hat factory workers. Mary would much rather have been home. John Derby, on the other hand, had little desire to be burdened by the company of a clinging wife when he was in Dedham.

By the end of May, tension was heavy in the Derby house, exacerbated no doubt by Anstis Townsend's ill-judged but well-meaning tendency to speak her mind when it came to her children's welfare. On May 23, John Derby reached the end of his very short tether and wrote an ultimatum to his mother-in-law:[75]

> *Hon^{d} Madam—*
>
> *I observe in your letter to Mary, expressions from which I infer, that you design to impress her mind with the idea, that she is unreasonably prevented visiting her home, by my authority.—It is not always convenient, to be attended by my wife & child in my rides to Dedham on business, & in certain situations of my family it would be highly improper.—Your*

> *condoling with her on a subject in which I consult my own interest, & of course hers, cannot but have a tendency to create dissentions in my family. I have no wish to circumscribe her filial duties,—but I will have her learn a lesson which it seems you have never taught her, that when her duty to her parents & to her husband meet in conflict, the last must always prevail. This is the law & the testimony.*
>
> *Besides, your efforts only defeat your object. For altho I designed to pass the court week with you, yet in consequence of your letter, I shall defer our visit to such a time, as she shall feel herself wholly indebted to my kindness for the favor & you appear disposed to receive me as something more than an unwelcome intruder.*

Despite his closing "Yours respectfully," Derby's letter was patently insulting. Its unmistakably cold tone dismissed her parents, and his vituperative punishment of Mary—preventing her from visiting them—announced a need to control his dependents even if he could not control his life.

The scene in the Derby house that preceded this letter can only be imagined. Had Derby opened his mother-in-law's note on the road from Dedham, arriving home already infuriated? Or did Mary, perhaps encouraged by her mother's words, complain at being left at home though the weather had turned mild and their daughter was healthy? There would have been no cold silence to this argument. Both Mary and John were outspoken, strong-willed. Did he hit her? Or just humiliate her, driving home his point that her family life was totally dependent on his whim and his judgment?

A month later, Mary was pregnant again.

* * * * * * *

The summer went on with little written down to chronicle the Derbys' disintegrating marriage. Horatio Townsend took a few days' road trip for his health, accompanied by Amy. Their circular loop through Marblehead, Salem, Andover and Medford gave Horatio a chance to visit with his old friend Colonel Pickman, who had first recommended John Barton Derby to his attention more than a decade previously. One can only guess that Derby may have been a topic of careful conversation.

In September, one of Mary's letters was carried to Dedham by John Derby's brother Elias, called Hasket. In later years, Hasket would become such an irritant to the Townsend side of the family that Mary declared, "We shall not tamely submit to any more of his <u>abominable impositions</u>."[76]

His early visits to the Derby household, and to his brother, drew him into the increasingly intense family situation. He bought a small house nearby, and five years later he married a local woman with whom he had three children, but Hasket apparently never adjusted to the work ethic of a rural landowner. In 1839, he mortgaged every piece of property he owned in Medfield to secure promissory notes for money he had borrowed from a Derby relative in Boston. The notes were not enough. His 1840 death record noted, succinctly, "suicide," while another account stated "hung himself."[77]

November then, and Amy's written record: "Nov 1822 Mother & Child returned to live at her Father's in Dedham." An event without obvious explanation: Mary was only halfway through her pregnancy; the winter was not yet severe; there is no suggestion that her father was suffering from a particularly severe period of illness. The fact that this was not a simple visit is underscored by Amy's phrasing of Mary coming "to live" and her placement of the record in the family register of significant events.

Mary and baby Sarah had left John Derby for good. She had chosen to put herself in a nearly untenable position: a married woman with one child, another on the way and a husband with whom she refused to cohabit. Most of the laws of the period were against her, but her family's love, connections and legal training saw her through the worst challenges of her new status, to a lifetime of respectability as Mrs. Derby of Medfield.

Making Do

The transition did not come without serious worries. On April 3, 1823, George Horatio Derby was born in Dedham, "child of Mary Townsend Derby"—no father listed on the birth record.[78] Not long after, Mary wrote of her two children to Aunt Sally: "I cannot feel as if I could ever part with them and I tremble for what may be their future lot in life."

She had reason to worry. John Derby was not one to give up without a fight, and real estate transactions between the two Derby brothers in 1822 and 1823 signaled that determination. A month after Mary returned to her family home in Dedham, John fired off his first salvo: he tried to lease Mary's property to his brother for farming purposes, on the grounds that Horatio's earlier bond only specified that Mary be allowed to "occupy and possess" the property on Frairy Street. Horatio fought back, making sure that the bond—which had previously just been kept in the family—was officially recorded at the Norfolk Registry. In that version of the document, Mary is specifically granted the right to occupy and "improve" the land—meaning that it was her right alone to farm the small village property, not John's.[79]

Apparently, this argument went on in the years that followed, Hasket (and, through him, John) remaining a thorn in the Townsend family's side. But John also had another reason to convey property to Hasket: he needed money to pay for room and board in Dedham now that he was no longer admitted into the Townsend house. The lease to his brother brought him a small semiannual payment. John improved on that in February 1823 by selling his other Medfield properties to Hasket as well. Thus, E. Hasket Derby, "Gentleman," became owner of an acre of land with a cottage on it and lessor of six additional acres of cropland—all directly adjacent to Mary Derby's house on Frairy Street.[80] Ironically, Derby family money was paying for this real estate—money still available to Hasket, if not to John.

In October 1823, Horatio converted his earlier bond into a deed for life that gave Mary the permanent protected residence she would need. Under conditions similar to a modern life tenancy agreement, the house was put in Mary's name with one stipulation: she could use the property during her lifetime however she chose but could not sell it outright because, at her death, the house on Frairy Street would become her children's inheritance from their grandfather. In other words, it was not legally Mary's property. Thus, John Derby could not claim any marital right to it.[81] By the end of the month, sister Lucretia reported to Amy, "Last week there was nothing done except getting our dear little George assigned to Mary."[82] Mary Derby had been granted custody of her children.

* * * * * * *

Having secured a permanent home for her family, Mary still had to contrive a way to support them. One of the solutions she hit upon harked back to an earlier generation of Frairy Street occupants: Patty Dwight and Jonathan Metcalf. Mary and her recently widowed friend Julia Butterfield[83] decided to go into business together, opening a shop in Medfield that catered to ladies. Its contents were never described, but it may have been designed as a hat shop. In 1825, Mary hired a carpenter on her parents' advice to "take one of the rooms and fix [it] up till we see how we make out," and another room was prepared for Julia to live in. "I should like to have her move in as soon as she can make it convenient," Mary continued, adding, in obvious reference to the Derby brothers, "she is aware of my reasons for not wishing the house to be open and exposed without her being there."

Mary hired a local man to plow the yard that stretched behind the house and barn, only cautioning him "that he must not plough up before the chaise house door as I should wish that to be left so that a chaise might be put in if necessary." Was she intending to grow a crop of rye for the preferred hat straw it produced? Or was she fighting back against the Derbys' continuing attempts to stake claim to the property? Hasket made himself as much of a nuisance as possible, even claiming a right to the manure that was to be used in Mary's yard. Throughout this time, Mary continued to live in Dedham or, for one period, with her aunts in Boston while she was apparently learning millinery. "I made two bonnets and a cap last week and my mistresses [who may have been her aunts] appeared satisfied with my progressing."[84]

The notion of this young, middle-class mother becoming a milliner was much more respectable than it might appear at first glance. The 1820s saw an explosion of hat manufacturing in Norfolk County as elsewhere in rural Massachusetts, where small-stream water power and good rye fields met. The earliest straw hat concerns functioned more as commercial middlemen than manufacturing plants. A merchant bought up and processed a load of straw and then literally "farmed it out" to rural families, especially women and girls, to braid into long plaits. The straw plaits were collected or turned in to the merchant-manager, who then oversaw their fabrication into some of the millions of hats, bonnets and caps worn by every man, woman and child in America. In time, Medfield would become a center of high-quality hat manufacture, with at least eight separate businesses established between 1801 and 1853. Ironically, the largest and best known of these, D.D. Curtis & Company, began in the North Street building constructed by young Reverend Jonathan Townsend back in 1747 and owned by the family until the mid-1800s.

But in 1825, the industry that would make Medfield famous was still in its early developmental stages, and there were opportunities for enterprising women like Mary Derby and Julia Butterfield to benefit from the diffuse manufacturing process. Whether Mary's time in Boston trained her as a hat maker or a trimmer, she was establishing an in-house commercial operation in Medfield that would provide income for her own family and respectable employment for other women short on funds.[85]

By early 1826, Mary had returned to Medfield to live, only to be summoned back to the family home in Dedham in late June. Horatio Townsend was dying.

Dedham July 10th 1826
My dear aunt,
Mrs. Butterfield is going to Medfield to be the bearer of the melancholy intelligence of the death of our dear father…he was releas'd from his mortal sufferings (which were great) this morning exactly as the clock struck two…when you come I should like to have you bring the dear boy there will be no one there to leave him with and I long to see him…
your afflicted niece
Mary[86]

During the first months after Horatio's death, the family's living arrangements remained the same: Anstis in the Townsend house in Dedham, Mary on Frairy Street, Aunt Sally on North Street and the two unmarried daughters, Amy and Lucretia, apparently on a peripatetic round among the households. Mary's shop was up and running, although no reports survive of its success. She was making the most of her urban family network: Aunt Lucretia Greene, living in Boston, sent city goods to Mary, including laces, muslin and boxes (presumably hatboxes), while Mary sent at least one bonnet to her aunt in return. When sister Lucretia was in Boston visiting, she was charged with buying and shipping thread to Medfield.

By the time the family's year of mourning came to an end, however, they had to confront the fact that widow Anstis was in a situation similar to Mary's a few years earlier. Anstis had a house to live in but she needed a source of income to maintain it and support herself. Over sixty years old, she was not about to set herself up in business like her daughter, so she made the next acceptable choice: Anstis leased part of the sizable Dedham house. At the same time, it was decided that Lucretia would permanently move to Frairy Street, where Amy was already staying with Mary, Sarah Anstis and George. The shuffling of goods, furnishings and family members caused quite a stir. Lucretia wrote: "How could you let Mr. F come with that little silly wagon? If he gets the things all on & safe there I shall think he does well. We were not in the least expecting him today."

This was followed by much less tidy penmanship. Anstis added:

we are in the utmost Confusion as you may well suppose loading a pleasure waggon with things enough for an ox team & not one rope. I have borrowd one piece & the Cord is a window cord & I beg you to send it all back by Sarah…[Mr F]*uller tells me that you have not got any hay, but he will*

> *get it from your uncle if you desire it and now my dear Mary will you let him get it, or must I have the poor old Creature* [their horse] *put out of the way*
> *hope to see you next week. I think you cant go to Boston to stay. I send a bag of Corn & meal for the fowles—your affectionate mother AT*[87]

From all external appearances, the house on Frairy Street, filling up with family, anchored a village property that must have appeared much like its neighbors'. An aging house stood on a two-acre lot with a barn that doubled as carriage house; a few chickens pecked around the backyard well; an elderly horse—too decrepit to pull a cart full of household goods—grazed in a small orchard of apples and pears. Only on the interior was the household less than typical, with its preponderance of female inhabitants, its small hat shop and a rambunctious four-year-old boy.

Love and Persistence

George Horatio Derby was a puzzle to everyone from the time he could talk. A later writer, reflecting on Derby's eventual success as a nationally famous humorist, offered one perspective on his boyhood:

> *When I first knew "John Phoenix" he was an apprentice in a cabinet factory, and the jolliest, most reckless and rollicking apprentice ever heard within its walls. No one could help liking him, and yet his employers were at their wits' ends to keep him from demoralizing* [distracting] *the whole corps of workmen. There was no end to his pranks and eccentricities as a boy, and you could hear his laugh ringing at all hours, and most often when restraint was most appropriate.*[88]

Other acquaintances remembered George—and his mother—somewhat differently. Mary was a "very witty and talented woman," one neighbor remembered, and her son took after her, but to an extreme. "He saw the ludicrous in everything and was always ready to make fun of everybody, regardless of age and position and, while people laughed at his wit, he was never a favorite and for the same reason, his mother was not." A classmate was more analytical and less amused: "He was decidedly aristocratic in his make-up, felt above his schoolmates, whom he made sport of in his pictures, which is probably the reason for his unpopularity."[89]

This teenage boy trying, and evidently not succeeding, at fitting into Medfield's traditional society had already survived the first of his mother's attempts to shape his character into a more seemly and less antisocial mold. When George was ten, he was sent to school on Thompson's Island in Boston Harbor. George spent three years at the School for Moral Discipline, an early experimental program for problem children run by Townsend family acquaintance and educator E.M.P. Wells. Behavioral rules were strict and expectations were high, and George did not fare well under the disapproving scowl of the Reverend Mr. Wells. From the first, he was homesick. Mary wrote in encouragement, sending cozy news from home: "I presume the 'old trees' are decked by your imagination in brighter hues than ever they were in reality…as for the house, and pond, your aunt, and I, we look pretty much the same…I have wish'd very much you could have some pears & shall send some."

During the school terms that followed, correspondence ran more to concerned exchanges between Mary and headmaster Wells on her son's progress: "I wish much to know your opinion of George and if you consider him improving and likely to (in any degree) answer our hopes and expectations." By 1836, the handwriting was on the wall. February's grade

House belonging to Mrs. M. Derby, signed "G.H.D." Pencil drawing by George Horatio Derby, circa 1835. *USMA Archives, George Derby Papers.*

report arrived in Medfield with oversized lettering in the comment section: "**Nothing favorable to report**," while a May letter elaborated, "He eggs others on to do bad things although he doesn't do so himself."[90]

George came home from the School for Moral Discipline to try another path in life. For six months in 1837, he worked as an apprentice to Colonel Oliver Felt, a cabinetmaker in neighboring Wrentham. Since this was the same period described in the "John Phoenix" reminiscence quoted above, it is not surprising that the apprenticeship did not last. Lucretia reported to Mary, who was visiting in Boston, that George was back in Medfield because the colonel was dissatisfied with him and had sent him home until he and his mother seriously reviewed the situation.

The succeeding months in his mother's house were painful. George was cause for constant worry. Worse yet, sixteen-year-old Sarah Anstis, dutiful and charming daughter, died suddenly three weeks after George's ignominious return. The cause of Sarah's death was not recorded, but its effect on Mary was so devastating that she left Medfield for a period of time to recover. "Found your Mother very pleasantly situated at Mr. Bowker's [in Walpole]," Lucretia wrote to George six months later, "quite at home and more contented than she was here; her mind does not dwell the whole time as it did at home upon her dreadful loss."[91]

While Lucretia watched over the Medfield property, George's next experiment was taking place in Andover, at the teachers' seminary that would become Phillips Andover Academy. Good grades, a quick mind and family connections got him admission and a working scholarship as secretary to schoolmaster W.A. Wells, whose eyesight was failing. Wells was a much more sympathetic man than his Moral Discipline relative, but even he had trouble figuring out how to solve the problem of George Derby. "I have never before found an occasion for the exercise of so great a share of judgment and caution in the management of any boy in my charge," Wells wrote cautiously to Mary. "He certainly possesses a most singular combination of superior attainments and unusual deficiencies, and of kindness and politeness with ill-manners and a forwardness sometimes bordering on impudence."

George's time in Andover did not last, and for the next four years, lack of family funds and lack of obedience kept him on the move. He tried teaching and store clerking and attended schools in Northfield, Massachusetts, and Norwich, Vermont. A biographer commented, "His mother's poverty had placed him in this most unfit position; her ambition saved him from it, and afforded a world of relief to his employers. She had energy to get a West Point cadetship."[92]

* * * * * * *

For whatever reason, independent and undisciplined George had developed an attraction to military life, and Mary, at wit's end in her attempts to see her only child become a contributing member of society—unlike his father—went far outside her comfort zone to help him. George's application was delivered to the U.S. Military Academy with letters of support from all the right people, including one from past president John Quincy Adams, a Harvard classmate of Mary's father. Eighteen of the most respectable men in Norfolk County, including ministers, judges, lawyers and businessmen, signed a testimonial in support of George's admission. The overlapping associations among these community leaders suggest that Mary may have had to ask only one gentleman directly for his support, knowing that he in turn would speak with colleagues of the Norfolk County bar, fellow worshippers at Dedham's Episcopal church, fellow board members of the Dedham Savings Bank and, of course, fellow classmates from Harvard College. William S. Hastings of the Ninth Congressional District wrote the most honest of the supporting documents. Of John B. Derby, Hastings said only that he "is now broken down in health and fortune," but the congressman went on to admire Mary Derby's determination following her "divorce": "In fact the son may be said to have been dependent on his mother's industry for his support and education."[93]

Mary Derby crafted the application's cover letter herself. Her determined daring, in addressing a group of unknown and important men; her deep love for George and sense of her own limited means; and her perspicacity in writing from the heart as only a mother could, all cloaked in a veil of humility, could not have failed to impress the admissions officers.

> *It is not proper for me to say much respecting his talents, but I have the honor to forward recommendations from the most respectable inhabitants of his own town, and from Dedham…*
>
> *I should not presume to address you upon any small or trivial concern; but I feel that the success of this application involves the interests and happiness of a beloved, (and now only) child to a degree which induces me to do what is very repugnant to my own feelings in thus forcing myself upon your notice.*
>
> *It has been the misfortune of my son never to have known the love and superintending care of a father: the anxiety and care which should be mutually sustained by both parents has devolved alone upon one and*

> *with the limited means I possess, I find it impossible to educate him as I could wish…*
>
> *There will be doubtless many other applicants but probably not one to whom this appointment would be of so much consequence.*[94]

Love and persistence finally succeeded. George graduated seventh in the famous class of 1846 with classmates including Stonewall Jackson and George McClellan, among other luminaries. The life of George "John Phoenix" Derby after that time has been thoroughly documented, including his heroism at Cerro Gordo during the Mexican War; his distinguished career as a topographical engineer in California and, later, in Florida; his brief brilliant career as one of America's foremost humorists; and his family life, decline into abstraction and death of an unspecified "brain disease" when he was only thirty-eight years old.[95]

Until the end, Mary continued to worry.

Photo of George Horatio Derby in uniform of topographical engineers, ca. 1846. *Bancroft Library Portrait Collection, Bancroft Library, University of California, Berkeley.*

In 1859, after it was clear that something was seriously wrong with George—he complained of failing vision and excruciating headaches, among other symptoms—he visited a specialist in Healing Springs, Virginia. What remains from this visit is the doctor's letter to Mary: "My impression is his disease is softening of the brain but I am glad to say that during his sojourn at this place his conduct was of a kind not to compromise him as an officer or a gentleman. I hope sincerely he may be restored to his wonted vigor."[96]

This was a letter answering Mary Derby's own direct questions, and those may be interpolated from the doctor's response. *What is the diagnosis of my son's ailments? Might he recover?* Then, sandwiched between the standard sickroom concerns, *Was he difficult?...is he lunatic?*

Throughout George's life, Mary had lived with the fear that her beloved son might degenerate into a copy of his father; that the willful, volatile wit and intelligence George had inherited from both sides of the family might turn selfish, spiteful and abusive, as they had in John Barton Derby. Letters from headmasters and employers, and later from advisors and colleagues, all spoke to the same concern and all provided a similar answer: "Whatever dissatisfaction he may have in his own mind I have not yet discovered anything like a disposition to make mischief by souring the minds of others."[97] George Horatio Derby died May 15, 1861, in New York, an officer and a gentleman to the end.

OUTLIVING JOHN

In the twenty years between George's appointment to West Point and his death in New York, life proceeded and changed in Medfield as well. Regrettably, much of the flow of Townsend-Derby letters that had documented the previous fifty years with such personal detail dried up, although correspondence between George, his mother and his wife, Mary Angeline Coons, continued and was carefully saved. These letters, however, had little to say about Medfield and much to say about the younger generation's life in California, Florida and New York. They belong to another story.

For this story, other nuggets of information loosely fit together in a picture of life at Mrs. Derby's, rather like an old photograph of the house in blurred reflection across Meetinghouse Pond.

First there was the changing cast of characters. After 1830, widow Anstis Townsend gave up living in Dedham. She moved to Medfield to live with her sister- and brother-in-law (Aunt Sally and Uncle Gregory) in the old Townsend family home on North Street. An unmarried niece lived there as well, tending to household chores and caring for Uncle Gregory, who was largely incapacitated. These Townsends were well along in years, in their late seventies and eighties, and their consolidation of three separate homes into one shared household was a practical solution to the limitations of advancing age.

Less than a block away, the younger generations lived in Mary's house on Frairy Street (or, as it was then known, the "road to Wheeler's Bottom"[98]). Mary had exchanged her accommodation of Julia Butterfield and Julia's young daughter for family life with sisters Sarah (Amy) and Lucretia; daughter Sarah Anstis until her death; and George Horatio between school episodes and apprenticeships. A man came by to do heavy outside work like digging up the garden and plowing the field. This female household was a period response to economic necessity and social propriety. Mary could not respectably rent out rooms to unmarried males, yet her own family with children made it difficult to find room for another entire family. In this case, Sarah and Lucretia provided a happy solution to the dilemma of no income. The two sisters each had small stipends from their father's will; Mary had a house and a small labor-intensive business; and living together brought the whole close-knit family back in proximity to share life, work and resources.

Aunt Sally Townsend, "Gentlewoman" and nominal matriarch of the family, was the first to die. In 1836, the contents of her will made it clear that she had been well-to-do. Anstis inherited her clothing. The three nieces were to divide up household furnishings and silver. Small bequests went to other relatives and friends. But Sarah's major concern was providing for Mary Derby and her children. This was a challenge, since John Barton Derby was still haunting the outskirts of her life and Hasket was just down the road, trying to manipulate his brother's financial interests. Sarah's solution was to put $3,000 in a trust fund "for the sole use and benefit of my niece Mary Derby," from which Mary would receive income every year. She could not touch the principal, though, until "the said Mary Derby shall be discharged from the bonds of matrimony with her present husband, by death or otherwise."[99] If or when that happened, the Derbys would lose all legal claim to any of Mary's property, and she would be financially, as well as matrimonially, free.

"By death or otherwise" proved to be much longer in coming than anyone would have predicted. After John Derby was summarily dismissed from the Townsend family and property, he remained in the Dedham area for a number of years, enlisting his brother in the effort to salvage some financial benefit from the failed union, and perhaps maintaining his law practice. More important to him, however, was his political faith in Andrew Jackson's campaign to become the seventh American president. One acquaintance remembered that Derby "was a politician of the class which may properly be styled the romantic school. He was a politician for the love of it."[100] Yet despite his devotion to the Jacksonian cause, a promised political appointment as customs surveyor for the port of Boston never came through, and Derby spent several years, instead, as a petty clerk in the surveyor's office.

View on Frairy St., one of a series of "Glimpses of Historical Medfield" by local photographer E. Chamberlain, circa 1890. Note the small cottage at the side of the Derby house. *Medfield Historical Society.*

Derby did not handle disappointment well. About 1835, he resigned his post, published an autobiographical pamphlet, *Political Reminiscences,* in which he excoriated everyone in Boston politics who was not a Jacksonian, and went mad. "I was sick," one of his later publications begins. "They said I had a brain fever. I saw fire flashing in my eyes like coruscations of lightning."[101] At the same time, he lost the use of his limbs. He was placed in a mental hospital for three years by relatives, and what is known of that time comes from another of the pamphlets that Derby wrote over the decade that followed. *Musings of a Recluse,* printed in 1837 after his release, is a compilation of original poetry and autobiographical sketches by which John Derby aimed to make some money as well as elicit sympathy for the impossible situation in which he found himself. The lead poem of the pamphlet was notable as one of the first public condemnations of institutional treatment for mental illness. Titled "The Victim of the Mad-House," it begins:

They shut him up; they bound him down
All in a darksome place;
They bathed, and cropped, and shaved his crown
And marked him with disgrace.

They lashed and drugged him o'er and o'er,
And laid him in the cold,
He slept upon an icy floor,
It made his heart grow old.

Derby further explained himself in a prose trailer to the poem: "Note: there is no opinion more false than that which now prevails in regard to the confinement of the insane. The hospital is for the benefit of the hard-hearted relatives of the sufferer, and not the sufferer. It relieves them from the performance of a great and imperative duty which they thus cast off and impose upon others. To the poor wretch, it is a sentence of doom."[102] In this and later pamphlets, the lawyer-turned-author repeatedly returned to a handful of primary themes. He gave thanks that the Lord had rescued him from his debilitating bout with mental and physical illness. He cherished the memory of his mother, who died when he was six, and his first wife ("My Wife, In Heaven!"). He denounced his family and acquaintances for abandoning him when he was down and out. He mourned his solitude and lack of loved ones. Never, in the eight of his small publications that still remain, did he acknowledge that his sainted first wife was followed by a second, unless the following stanza from a poem titled "Spleen" may be taken to describe his ill-fated marriage to Mary:

How oft, on winter's night the fire
Of sacred home, burns fierce with ire?
How oft, the couch of wedded bliss
Is frighted by thy venomed hiss;
Ye lurk within each joyous hour,
Like hornet in a fragrant flower[103]

More surprisingly, Derby's writings never mentioned George Horatio either. One poem even asserted, "ne'er a Son—to carry down/ My name, among the throngs of fellow men!"[104] Perhaps coincidental but more likely not, Derby's denial echoed that of his wife nineteen years earlier, when George's birth was baldly recorded as "child of Mary Townsend Derby."[105] The two tried hard not to exist for each other.

John Barton Derby continued to live in Boston until 1867, known throughout the region both by his reputation as having once had promise and for his later appearance and behavior. A correspondent for the *Hartford Press* prepared a reminiscence of him that reads like a child's cautionary tale, concluding:

> *He spent his days on the State Street sidewalks and in the offices of that locality, in sight of those who had known him under better fortunes, and who aided him sometimes by direct contribution, and often by purchases of articles that he would vend…He was the wreck of a man in appearance for a long time, but had reached the age of seventy-six at the time of his death.*[106]

****

As long as John Derby was alive, Aunt Sally's will only served to remind Mary of the persistent consequences of a foolish marriage. Adding to the injury, another aunt left her a bequest with the same stipulation.[107] Mary made what effort she could to undo the problem. In 1842, with George about to depart for West Point, she consulted with Theron Metcalf, an old family friend and Massachusetts Supreme Court justice who had written one of George's recommendations. Did Judge Metcalf think that her marriage to John B. Derby had actually been legal? After all, they exchanged vows

before a temporary minister who was only filling in because the Dedham Episcopal church had dismissed its rector in 1818. Could her marriage be respectably annulled? Metcalf regretfully replied that the marriage vows were legal.[108]

Mary's inability to touch the inheritance that should be hers, combined with Uncle Gregory's death in 1840 and George's need to be outfitted at considerable expense for West Point, precipitated the next transformation of the Frairy Street house. Mother Anstis sold the large family home in Dedham—the "castle" where the girls had grown up. She sold the Reverend Townsend house in Medfield where she must have been rattling about after the deaths of Sarah and Gregory, and she moved in with her daughters. At the same time, the Townsend ladies took in Sarah Adelaide Moore, a young teenage relative from Vermont. "Addie," as she was called, reminded Mary of her own daughter, and in later years the older woman treated her as such. Addie could learn from the Townsend clan and be sheltered by them while contributing young legs and a strong back to the household.

It was past time to seriously update the building, now needing to accommodate five adult women and an occasional family visitor. The money from selling two houses likely funded the renovations, for it was Anstis's, Sarah's and Lucretia's inheritance. No documents remain to date the construction work or to tell whether the changes happened all at once or bit by bit over ten or twenty years. Stylistic details, recycled timbers, paint layers and artifacts do identify what was accomplished, however, during the mid-1800s.

The most visible changes came on the outside. A connector shed was built between the house and the barn that provided a dramatic increase in comfort and privacy. No more slogging a muddy sixty feet from the kitchen's back door, past the well to the side barn entrance. The women could now walk dry and discreetly to feed the chickens, retrieve stores or visit the privy attached to one side of the barn. The shed had many uses. In the end closest to the kitchen, a small coal stove near the well provided heat and water for a summer kitchen, allowing the house interior to stay cool on muggy July days when there was bread that needed baking or jam to be boiled. At the barn end, they finally had the dry storage that was never guaranteed in the cellar.[109]

Meanwhile, the east end of the house was also undergoing renovation. A two-story addition was tacked on to the side, expanding what had been a small "buttery" downstairs, plus an equally small upper chamber, into two reasonably large and delightfully sunny rooms. Upstairs, there would be a bedroom for one of the sisters. Downstairs, Mary set up a music room, which doubled as a comfortable back parlor.

Two dormers were cut into the roof, giving light and a view of the millpond to the attic. Plank partition walls were erected to roughly define a room at each end of the space—one of them, perhaps, for Addie Moore.[110] The carpenters did more than cut holes in the roof. Long reinforcing strips of heavy lath were attached on the inside to allow for a dramatic improvement: the whole house was reroofed, not with cedar shakes, but with roofing slates. This one change, more than any other, was a declaration of status, pride and respectability. Of course, it was also more fireproof[111] and probably more weathertight. But the newly remodeled, newly painted, slate-roofed building by the pond must have been as noteworthy to neighbors and passersby as Seth and Hannah Dwight's "new" house had been a century earlier. Mrs. Derby's house, standing on the edge between working-class Frairy Street lodgings and a whole new developing neighborhood along North Street, clearly stated where its allegiance belonged.

Probably at this time, Mary ended whatever business she still had going. The front parlor that had served as shop and workroom was formally returned to domestic use by removing its separate side entrance and inserting a window instead. Coal grates were installed in the fireplaces. The vast kitchen fireplace opening—an inefficient and drafty relic of Hannah Dwight's tenure in the early 1700s—was walled in, leaving only a single small round hole for the stovepipe that vented a modern coal and wood cookstove. Lucretia, in charge of cooking and baking, must have been delighted once she learned to control the new appliance.

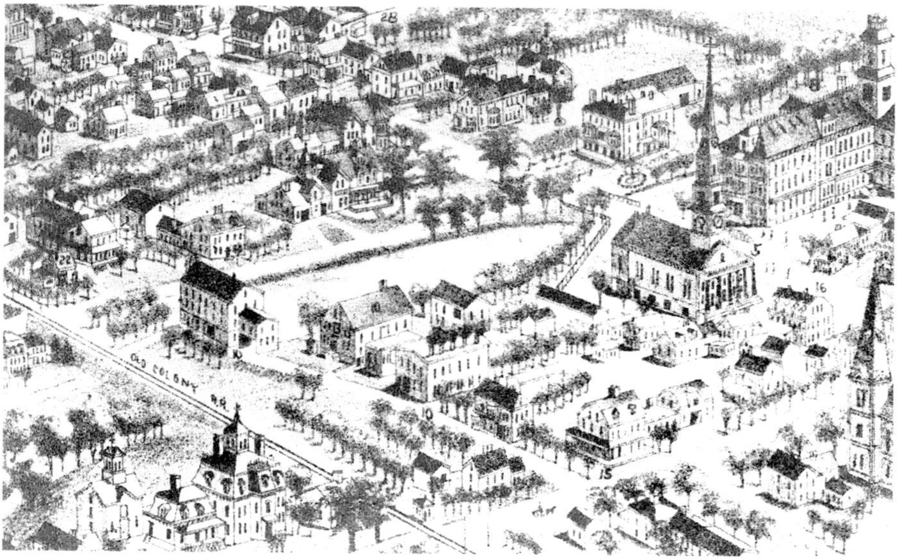

Frairy Street area from "Medfield Massachusetts 1888," a bird's-eye view lithograph by (C.?) H. Bailey & Co., Boston. From a later print by Medfield Historical Society.

Anstis Townsend was the next Frairy Street resident to depart, dying during the winter of 1850 after eighty-five years in Medfield and Dedham. This nearly invisible woman who rarely appeared in the family's letters was still a treasured part of George Derby's boyhood. So two years later, on a visit home from his western expeditions, he honored her memory by crafting a classic Victorian mourning poem—a rare bit of serious writing for the humorist. Descriptive passages recreate the midcentury atmosphere of the house on Frairy Street.

I sit in my grandmothers chamber,
In her high backed easy chair
And I think on the days departed
When the kind old lady sat there.
Through the open casement is floating
The syringa's rich perfume
And the pictures she loved to gaze on
still hang on the walls of the room…

Everything else is unaltered
her knitting lies in my hand

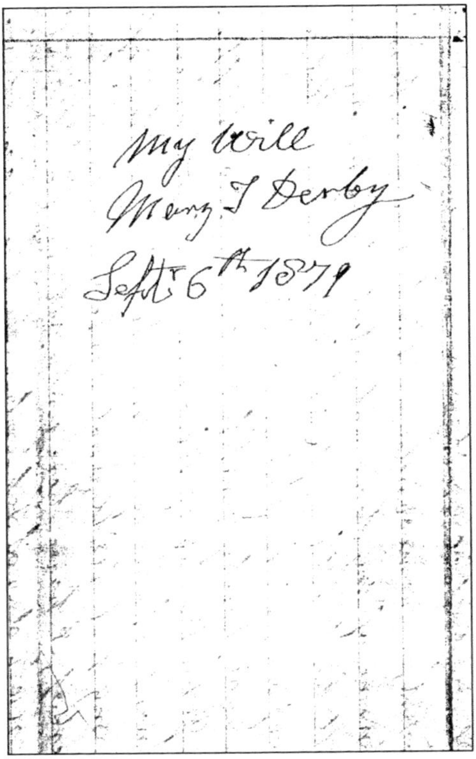

My Will
Mary T Derby
Sept 6th 1879

"My Will"; manuscript page in Mary Derby's handwriting, 1879. *Norfolk County Register of Probate.*

And her bible and prayer book
are there too
on the small old fashioned
stand
But her clock as it ticks in the
chamber
from twilight until dawn
Seems always sadly repeating
she is gone forever gone—[112]

In 1854, Sarah Townsend also left the house, marrying a judge in Washington, D.C., about whom nothing is known except his name—Ezra Williams—and the fact that he died in 1861. Did Sarah return to the Frairy Street house for eight years until she, too, died? Her name, with her husband's, is on the Derby family monument in Medfield's Vine Lake Cemetery, but so is that of George Horatio Derby, whose body is interred at West Point.[113]

The last years of Mary Derby's life must have been much quieter and more tranquil than her youth. When George died in 1861, she was sixty-four years old, Lucretia was sixty-three and Addie Moore was twenty-two. Over the next two decades, Mrs. Derby and Miss Townsend maintained a respectable and (part of the respectability) largely unnoteworthy presence in Medfield. They provided meeting space in their parlor for the Baptists at one point, according to local lore. A local paper commented on her "rare conversational powers."[114] Mrs. Derby was finally relieved of her scandalous marriage in 1867 and, ironically, became a wealthy widow—thanks in no way to her husband, but to her own family inheritance. The sisters' property included land and buildings on both Frairy and North Streets, where they lived in a mixed neighborhood of farmers, laborers and the town's preeminent straw hat manufacturer, Daniel Curtis. The Derby house was full of elegant if old-fashioned furnishings inherited from Uncle Gregory and Aunt Sally as well as from their parents, and

Mary's bank account finally included the monetary bequests for which she had waited over thirty years.

By 1879, Addie Moore had truly become part of the family. The census-taker listed her position in the family as "adopted daughter" who was "keeping house," while a younger Irish girl was the household's "servant."[115] Mary, still careful to protect and support those for whom she felt responsible, wrote out a will carefully detailing her provisions for Addie and Lucretia Townsend.[116] To her "beloved sister" and to "Sarah Adelaide Carpenter Moore, also of Medfield, my daughter by love, and adoption, (though through no legal form)," she left all of her income and dividends for their mutual support until such time as Lucretia died.

Mary carefully listed the furnishings she wanted Addie to keep, perhaps concerned that others might doubt the younger woman's right to them or perhaps simply reminiscing as she wrote.

> *I give to my adopted daughter, SAC Moore,...a portion of my furniture, & effects as follows—*
>
> *1 bedstead, feather bed, bolster & pillows, that are in her chamber, and one hair mattress, also, one feather bed marked W—and all the rest of the furniture, contained in her apartment, save one small Bureau—The Easy chair that belonged to my beloved mother,*[117] *one Cabinet Chair, my work table—and desk, with contents, standing in my chamber closet, Screen standing in front Entry, picture of Star King, all my Harpers magazines bound or unbound, looking glass in keeping room, my travelling Trunks & valese, little table, that belonged to my friend Miss Olive Perry, and chair of the same—My small old Piano, the large one belongs to her, as I bought it, and gave it to her, but in case of any dispute about it, I hereby ratify the gift, also I give her the music stool—The chest of drawers standing in my chamber which we call the Jumping Jenny—1 rug that we worked together, & one small one worked in flowers—one wooden table which stands in the Attic chamber—1 dozen bottles Currant wine—one dozen cups and saucers, white, and with handles (in the Side Board) one round card table, a small rocking chair, and the chair usually occupied by me in the Sitting room, and an old fashioned chair with Castors*[,] *the light stand, which stands by the side of my bed, & a round table that is in the parlor with pictures pasted on it—*

The list literally furnishes a middle-class Victorian domestic environment, offering a unique glimpse inside the Dwight-Derby House. Unique also are the glimpses of Mary Derby and her family—making currant wine, hooking a woolen rug, working at the writing desk, hosting musicales, reading aloud from *Harper's Weekly* as she sat in her favorite chair.

Mary's will was about more than reminiscing, however. As matriarch of the Townsend-Derby clan, she still needed to provide for her younger sister and see her settled in her last years. The Frairy Street house was, finally, not Mary's to give or keep due to her father's cagey planning of sixty years before. It would go to George's three children, and she did not know them very well. Would they immediately try to sell it when she was gone? She wrote the next part very carefully, showing both ladylike entreaty and an iron will to reach beyond the grave:

> *As my right in the homestead ceases at my decease, and will become the Inheritance of my three Grand children,…I earnestly entreat of them, to allow my Sister Lucretia…to occupy such portions of the house & premises as she may require,…rent free…so that she may have a home in her old age…But if they refuse to accede to this my request, my will is, that they shall not come into possession of any portion of my Estate…for five years, after the decease of the said Lucretia.*

Mary Townsend Derby, portrait photo circa 1850. *USMA Archives, George Derby Papers.*

In the end, she need not have worried. "Mrs. M.T. Derby, well-known in this section, died, at her residence on Frairy Street, Saturday, September 11th, of cholera morbus, after a short illness."[118] Less than two weeks later, before her will was even probated, Lucretia Townsend also died.

The *Norfolk County Gazette* characterized Mary Derby as "a lady of great intelligence, [with] talents of a high order." One of those talents was making a two-hundred-year-old house usable for seventy years to come.

CHAPTER 4

The Inheritors

1880–2009

AHA! MOMENT: THE WELL

From the start of Medfield's interest in the Dwight-Derby property, archaeology was always an important part of the research mix. It had helped that Medfield's town historical commission included an Archeology Advisory Committee, a mixed bag of professionals and amateurs, geologists and antique collectors who kept an eye on municipal improvements and private developers, and relished any chance to get their hands dirty. It also helped that a whole generation of Medfield children had grown up knowing that archaeology happened in their own backyards. For years, every seventh grader had taken part in an interdisciplinary circus fondly known as the "Never-ending Dig."[119] And for years their parents and siblings and neighbors had been drawn into the project, resulting in town-wide support and an enthusiastic cheering squad for archaeological research.

In 1996, one of the first explorations of the Dwight-Derby property was done with ground-penetrating radar equipment—a technology primarily used in oil exploration at the time. Geologist John Thompson had convinced Hager-Richter Geosciences to scan the Medfield lot for free, as a way of exploring new applications for its equipment. The scientists arrived on a raw, damp morning and for the next two hours tromped back and forth, crisscrossing the yard as they dragged a sled full of equipment behind them. A week later, we were presented with charts representing a radar

IAC archaeologists test the front yard for evidence of past lives, 1998.

scan of soil layers and anomalies below the ground's surface. There had been some problems in the testing, including dampness and the small scale of the experiment; information on the charts was difficult for laypersons like us to understand. In the end, the scans were conclusive only about what was *not* there: there was no evidence of foundations and, more surprising, no evidence of a well. Surely the Dwights and Derbys had a well.[120] In fact, there was even a letter from the 1890s discussing the well running dry. Could it possibly have been dug so far away from the house that it was outside present lot lines?

We had a second try at answering that question in 1998 and 1999, when a more traditional archaeological dig took place. By then, the house was on the National Register of Historic Places and subsurface testing was required before any work could be done that disturbed the ground. Since two of the most vital house repairs included repointing the entire foundation and replacing almost 80 percent of its sills, a team from Independent Archaeological Consulting (IAC) was hired to survey the building perimeter. Focusing on corners and doorways and other likely well-used spots, the IAC team excavated tidy squares and rectangles, expanding them when a promising feature emerged, scraping out layers of fill, soil, nails, brick bits and charcoal until they reached the bottom of human disturbance around the house. They tested areas away from the foundation as well, partly to see what "normal" Derby yard topography looked like and partly to explore promising bumps and hollows for signs of the missing well.[121]

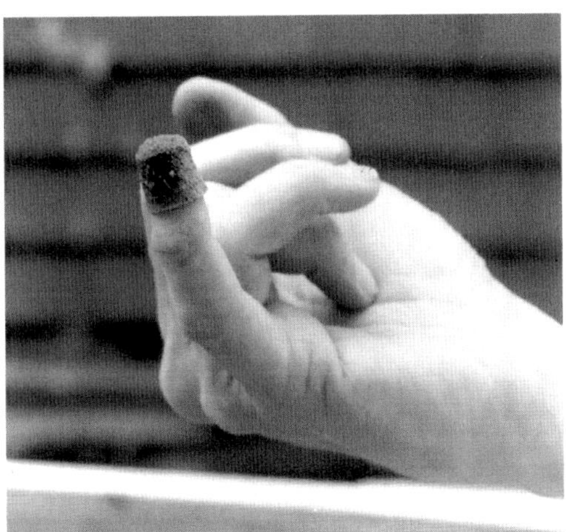

Archaeological treasure: a nineteenth-century thimble.

No well appeared. The crew found remnants of an abandoned water pipe cutting across the backyard—evidence of the earliest town waterline installed. They found stone footings for what may have been a porch or lean-to outside the east parlor where Jonathan Metcalf and, later, Mary Derby may have run their shops. The ten thousand artifacts that they unearthed identified building materials for more than one phase of house construction, suggested changing trash disposal practices and "furnished" the kitchen and dining room with popular glass and ceramic styles.

Occasionally a single artifact would stand out—a storyteller among the mass of data. One lone stone spear, called a Merrimac point, reminded us of hunters whose territory extended along Vine Brook 5,500 years before Timothy Dwight claimed a patch of it for himself. A shiny blue-decorated, gray-glazed ceramic shard linked New World with Old, by way of a German drinking mug that John Dwight might have used. An innocuous but lethal-looking two-tined fork with a bone handle called up one of the Townsend ladies at work in the kitchen. Fragments of everyday life, the artifacts gave texture to the smooth-featured past. None of them was more evocative than a small thimble, buried outside the west parlor window. "I wish you to get me a thimble dear S[arah] one of those 20 cent ones if you can, you know about how large I want it, don't get it too large if your finger goes to the bottom I should think it would be about right."[122]

Part of what the IAC excavations confirmed was that the Dwight-Derby yard, like the house itself, had gone through centuries of renovations. Building and repair trenches had been dug outside the walls. Holes had been dug for pipes and fence posts. Walks had been laid, trees planted and removed and old driveways resurfaced. Regretfully, we resigned ourselves to the fact that the old well either lay under a thick layer of asphalt or had been abandoned and so thoroughly filled in a century ago that it had become invisible.

Fortunately, stabilizing the building did not require finding a well, and the next three years were absorbed by massive renovation activities, from basement to the top of the crumbling chimney. As the essential house work was completed, plans were already forming to reconstruct a dilapidated breezeway that connected house to barn. The structure had few obvious historic elements—a concrete pad with torn screen walls and a sagging roof—and was judged not worth repairing. Its location would be perfect, however, for a proper visitors' entry and gathering space adjacent to the fragile old house.

In April 2002, the backhoe arrived. I took quick photos of demolition in progress (bites taken out of the roof, clouds of dust as rafters gave way) and headed back to work. Late that afternoon, John Thompson, chair of the Archeology Advisory Committee, called. "Hey, Electa, guess what? I just heard from Doug Whitla." Doug was a Friends member and local builder who was supervising the breezeway project. "You won't believe this. They found the well!"

"What do you mean, they found the well? Where?"

"The backhoe guy was breaking up the old concrete floor—it was right underneath! So he left it alone and dug a couple of test holes by the barn, but Doug wants to know if we want to take a look before they dig the rest of the foundation?"

It wasn't really a question of wanting or not wanting to look. The same restrictions applied to the breezeway as to the rest of the house: we were legally required to conduct archaeological testing under the terms of the property's preservation restriction. Somehow that detail had gotten lost, it turned out, both in scheduling and budgeting for the project. The backhoe was supposed to complete its work in two more days, and there was no money to hire an archaeologist.

A series of frantic phone calls, negotiations and applications resulted in a workable Plan B. The excavator went away, his return engagement scheduled for July 1. The Massachusetts Historical Commission gave approval for an "emergency data recovery" to be conducted under the supervision of Frederica Dimmick, a National Park Service archaeologist who volunteered her time to the project. And members of the Medfield Archeology Advisory Committee finally got a chance to get our hands dirty. We had nine days, after hours and on weekends, to gather all the information possible from this site that was about to be destroyed, and make sense of an area that had been in constant use for three hundred years.

A couple of factors made the challenge easier. The well, focus of excitement and controversy, would not actually be excavated. While this was vastly disappointing, it was the only reasonable choice for a group of informed but inexperienced amateurs. Architect David Sharff adjusted building plans so that the ground around the well could be left alone. Only the top two courses of stone would have to be removed, high above the well's depths and probably above any significant artifact deposit. The new room overhead would have a trapdoor to provide access for someone, sometime, with the skill and resources to do justice to this feature.

Elsewhere in the space, the early backhoe test digging had created rough-and-ready pits and large dirt piles waiting to be sifted for artifacts. Fortunately, these were in the least sensitive part of the site, near the barn/carriage house. That left the kitchen doorway and well perimeter for the seven of us to concentrate on.

We began with an unexpected bonus: a thick layer of sand that covered the entire space. It had been laid down in the 1950s as a leveling bed for the concrete pad poured over it. But it had functioned like a layer of packing peanuts: padding whatever lay beneath it, protecting the artifacts from being

Pressed glass "peg" lamp found under the breezeway floor. Peg lamps, inserted in candlesticks, were used in the early nineteenth century when whale oil was introduced for lighting.

crushed. Concrete and sand together had formed an impervious seal over the archaeological deposits, and their removal exposed materials that in normal circumstances do not survive in New England.

Our hurried excavations did not find the seventeenth century.[123] We actually found very little that could be assigned with any assurance to the Dwights. We did find a few whole items and a lot of architectural debris likely associated with Townsends and Derbys, from cut nails and roofing slates to a simple glass fixture known as a peg lamp, designed as a candlestick insert when oil replaced tallow for lighting. We found that the ground from the back door to the well was packed from use, while the area between the well and barn was less heavily trodden. We also discovered remnants of supports for a wooden floor under the original summer kitchen that the breezeway had replaced, and we imagined Mary and Lucretia's pleasure at having an indoor source of water on miserable winter days.

Most important to us, however, was a whole group of finds that we had not even expected. Under the breezeway, packed in the sand and along the edge of the barn, were clues to the lives and activities of people for whom there is almost no paper documentation: the renters who lived in Mary Derby's house for seventy years after she died, whose trash would be cleared out by Edith Baker's construction crew.

Genteel Decay...

> *Medfield Jun 14 1890*
> *Mr Derby:*
> *Dear Sir: I received from James Ord last Sept. a request to collect arrears of rent on the Derby houses which I have done & rents due to this date and render the enclosed statement.*
> *Mr. Hamilton the occupant of the old house has removed the fence in front of the house. This is becoming the fashion here no fence in front.*[124]

Ten years after Mary Derby's death, Ralph Battelle began his tenure as property manager of the Derby estate. The job included collecting rents from tenants in three buildings: the "old house" and "cottage" on Mary's lot, and the "Frairy Street house," which may have been the cottage across the way once owned by John Derby's brother Elias Hasket. Battelle contracted for and supervised needed repairs and carried on long-distance discussions with Captain George McClellan Derby, George Horatio's son and managing heir of the estate.[125] A few of Battelle's reports to Derby survive, providing glimpses of old house maintenance challenges.

The small "Frairy Street house," rented by William Crawford, was having tenant problems in 1890. "The abutters on both sides," Battelle reported, "complain of so much stock kept in a door yard and wish some change could be made." While this was still part of the estate as late as 1905, nothing more is known about it or its inhabitants. Work on the "old house" and the cottage was ongoing in the meantime, ranging from repairing the kitchen pump to repointing chimneys and painting the exterior. The kitchen ceiling in the cottage was near collapse and had to be replastered for fire prevention as well as aesthetic reasons.

These jobs were seen to fairly quickly, but Captain Derby was reluctant to spend money on the barn. In 1891, Battelle had written:

> *If it is repaired there will have to be new sills all round, some sleepers; barn leveled up; some new plank for floor; new doors & casings; roof shingled and sides patched. One man has offered to do it for $150...A new barn about the same size would cost about $350, for carpenter and painter work and there would be grading besides. If you do anything I think it better to repair as outlined above.*

But a year went by and the barn had still not been mended. Battelle changed his mind: "It seems to me the barn is not worth repairing that the money laid out on it would be thrown away and it would be better to build a new one."

No further correspondence about the barn survived, but the building in its present condition attests to generations of continued patching and making do. Some of the support posts for the first floor are sawn red oak in beautiful condition, but with empty mortises that indicate that they were recycled from an earlier building; others are worm-eaten whole or half-round tree trunks. One whole side of the two-bay structure had the ceiling raised at a later date to accommodate a high-cab truck or auto, but the work was done piecemeal with miscellaneous timbers; footing repairs consisted of replacing rotten post ends with chunks of sawn timber, barely attached to the frame above. By the time Medfield purchased the Frairy Street property, the barn's condition exactly matched Battelle's description of a century earlier. The fact that it survived to be rescued yet again is a minor miracle.

One further Battelle report moved the main house toward twentieth-century convenience:

> *Medfield Sept. 12 1894.*
> *Mr. Derby:*
> *Dear Sir: Owing to the unusually dry season the water at the old house has given out entirely and I am requested to supply it by putting in the town water. It will cost about $51.00 to put it into the house and $10 per annum for the water rent of one faucet, thereafter.*

> *I ask your instruction with regard to it. I think Hamilton will stay for the present and they are a good tenant & the pay is promptly made and it is desirable to keep them.*
>
> *Yours truly, R.A. Battelle*

Indoor plumbing, of sorts, had come to the Dwight-Derby house, and the ancient well was on its way to demolition.

Improvements to Medfield's public works were not limited to piped water. The 1880s also began an extended period of downtown gentrification, encouraged by a national village beautification movement and largely underwritten, apparently, by E.V. Mitchell, whose straw works dominated the town and whose sprawling Queen Anne–style house abutted the Derby property. In 1885, Frairy Street was widened, and the functional millpond across from the Curtis and Derby tenants was tidied up with a neat stone wall surrounding it. At the dam across the lower end, Baker and Cushman's carriage plant still identified the scene as a manufacturing locale, but the plant buildings were new and freshly painted, like those of the straw works. Meanwhile, the white-steepled church, Derby house and Curtis house lent graciousness to the scene. Three years after Baker's Pond—now coming to be known as Meetinghouse Pond—was walled in, E.V. Mitchell paid to install a fountain near the east end. The graceful spray of water was a gesture of civic pride, although citizens at the time probably commented on its proximity to Mitchell's own house and that of his in-laws and reminded each other of the recent brouhaha when Mitchell's factory had polluted the pond with dye.[126]

A few scraps of information have filtered down about the families who rented the Derby house.[127] Mr. Hamilton, who removed the front fencing in 1890, was elsewhere referred to as E.H. Hamilton. He had a family; they were good tenants and paid their rent on time. Following their tenancy, the house was perhaps occupied by James Ord, by George Osborne and by R. Crawford and his three sons from Nova Scotia.[128] There may have been other lodgers as well, renting only a single room or staying in the cottage out back, since Medfield's population expanded every winter and summer during the hat factory's busy seasons.

The Great Depression may have emptied the house of its tenants, leaving it vulnerable to increasing numbers of homeless tramps who rode the rails only a block away. Perhaps the owners worried at the increasing number of foreigners populating Frairy Street.[129] Whatever the impetus, the remaining Derby heirs decided to sell the family homestead. Another generation had taken over property management, and in 1934, Margaret Black wrote to her eighty-year-old uncle George McClellan Derby, telling him that a For Sale sign had gone up.

> *I shall certainly hate to see the old place go from the family but I suppose it is the only wise thing to do as it will be increasingly expensive to keep up as it grows older, and as Medfield is so inaccessible it seems improbable that anyone in the family will ever care to live there. I can see no great rise in value in the land itself as Mr. Wheeler says one acre brings about $300 in Medfield, and with no direct railroad from Boston the growth will be slow.*[130]

The Derby house and grounds described in the advertisement would generally be familiar to a visitor today. For the historian, the ad roughly dates some building improvements and confirms the presence of other features. In May 1934, the Dwight-Derby House sat on a little over an acre of land. "Early Colonial, painted yellow, clapboards and slate roof. Large central chimney. Southern exposure." The yellow color chosen by popular vote in 1998 was not a recent fashion.[131] On the other hand, the shingles now covering the south and west walls of the house apparently came later. Inside, first-floor rooms and fireplaces were unchanged, with a "den, kitchen and laundry" across the back matching the present shop, great room and kitchen, respectively. There was no massive hearth in the 1934 kitchen, this having been walled up in Mary Derby's day. "Cook by coal. Boiler at kitchen stove." Upstairs the same four bedrooms, two with fireplaces, existed then as do today, although the ad goes on to acknowledge only "1 bathroom and one room suitable for second bathroom." A second bath would not be added until the 1960s, to accommodate the Harris family with their two children. Two separate rooms existed in the attic, only one being finished—presumably the west end with its unusual gambrel ceiling.

There was a furnace, electricity, town water and sewer. The shed and barn needed shingling again. "Grounds: Good for gardens. Some good old trees. Pond across road. Quiet environment. Well-to-do neighbors. Sale price: $6,000 cash. Rent: $25 a month." To which was added in pencil: "not bringing that now."

Either the advertising was a failure or else Margaret and her husband, Roger Derby Black, changed their minds. They held onto the property until Roger died in 1942. Margaret then moved into the old Frairy Street house herself, the sole occupant for three years, perhaps fixing it up yet again or possibly just keeping it in one piece until it was sold in 1945, to a Dedham woman who turned it over to friends three years later.[132] The Baker family, especially Mrs. Edith Baker, was responsible for the next incarnation of the house on Frairy Street.

...and Colonial Revival

The Dwight-Derby House would remain in private hands for another fifty years before the town bought it. Most of one family would vacation there; a second would raise children, survive divorce and manage life in an ancient house that had many drawbacks and that, like most old houses, did not take well to modern methods of improvement.

Of all those who spent time at the Frairy Street property, Edith Clifford Prescott Baker had the greatest impact. She moved to Medfield as an older woman, having raised four children in Brookline with her husband, Theodore "Ted" Baker, who owned a well-known Ford dealership there. In 1948, a year after Mr. Baker's death, Edith sold their Brookline home and moved into the Medfield house recently purchased from Dedham acquaintances. Apparently, she had first learned of the property from family friend Evelyn Byng, who lived in an equally historic homestead on Wight Street. Edith was "excited and full of energy," one of her daughters remembered, "and we, her four children...were just as pleased."[133]

Assisted by an unidentified architect and what must have been a substantial crew of workmen, Edith Baker threw herself into the repair and rehabilitation of the Dwight-Derby House. The work she oversaw was a combination of architectural restoration—removing selected nineteenth-century features to return the building and its grounds to a more "colonial" look and feel—and internal modernization to make the building habitable by twentieth-century standards.

Mary Derby's Victorian kitchen went away. A compact modern kitchen was installed in the small west room. The coal-heated cookstove in the great central room was carted off. Plaster came down, and in what must have been a thrilling moment, the vast Dwight hearth and chimney piece came to light again. It was not in good condition: a new mantel needed to be set over the opening and the chimney wall faced with new boards; crumbling bricks around the interior were replaced. Wide boards were found to replace the worst of the flooring. Chances are that the chimney was repointed, at least above roof level, so the fireplace could once again be used for winter blazes. The "keeping room," as Edith called it, was stripped of paint, in accordance with then current understanding of colonial interior decoration.[134] Elsewhere, rich paint colors were chosen, like the peacock blue used for a guest room (afterward known as "the Peacock Room"), while a scenic wallpaper resembling French *toile* lent elegance to the front stairwell.

In some places, colonial had to give way to modern. A furnace installed in the cellar required a maze of ductwork to move warm air upstairs. New screens were needed, new piping and a new claw-foot tub to replace the zinc-lined wooden box in the bathroom. The old box tub was saved as a conversation piece in the barn loft, where it still sits today.

When the interior was basically finished, Edith Baker turned her attention to the outside, which needed almost as much attention. Like the main kitchen, Mary Derby's summer kitchen ell behind the house was an anachronism, so Edith transformed it into a different kind of summer room. Trash that had been cleared from the cellar and attic, perhaps just dumped out back to be dealt with later, was leveled and covered in sand: a boy's broken arrow, a bisque doll face, a salt cod box, old paint brushes, medicine bottles, a ruby glass dish, a strap hinge and an iron key from a replaced door. Concrete was poured to replace the rotting wood floor; the roof was reinforced and shingled yet again; flat wall-boarding was replaced with sturdy screens. The result was a breezeway big enough for grandchildren to play in and cool enough for guests to relax in during summer's hottest days. While the masons were at it, they laid a concrete pad inside the rickety barn as well, so at least the Baker Fords would not disappear through the floorboards.

Gardens came next, and with them lots of yardwork. Old-fashioned shade plants for the west side of the property—bleeding hearts, violets, lilies of the valley, hostas, peonies. Lilacs trimmed at the house corners; ornamental cherry and dogwood in the east yard. Likely a lot of brush was cleared, a lot of pruning done to the good-sized pines and the great oak that dominated the landscape. A few gnarled apple trees were saved, heirlooms from an earlier time. White picket fencing defined the building's private space and kept young charges away from the road, closing off the driveway on one side and defining a backyard on the other. A careful curve of yew hedged the front yard and softened the effect of old house geometry.

Then it was time for sharing the pleasures of life in Medfield with family. "All of us spent a lot of time with our mother in that house," daughter Augusta recalled. "Most of the grandchildren were old enough to develop the same fondness and love for her and the house that we had. With six bedrooms she had room for all of us. The kids explored every inch and found endless places to hide playing games such as 'sardines in the box.'"

Though they weren't allowed in the attic at all, her son remembered:

> *We fished and skated on the pond. We swam in "gingerale water" at the Jewell's and Goldthwait's. We skied and picnicked at Rocky Woods. Occasionally we dined at Francis Cafe around the corner. The family parties, with the help of Mary Mair Etienne (Hardy), were glorious affairs, not to be forgotten, lobster salad on Christmas Eve and roast beef or lamb from the market on North Street.*[135]

From a child's perspective, Christmas Eve meant a crèche set up in the opening of Hannah Dwight's old bake oven. Exploring included playing with an old wheeled sled in the barn and believing that the eighteenth-century storage space by the chimney led to a secret passage somewhere deep in the house.[136]

The Dwight-Derby House gave a new lease on life to Edith Baker, and she gave one to it in return. Fifteen years later, when Chester and Jane Harris bought the Frairy Street property in 1963, they purchased an up-to-date antique. The Harris family lived there for over three decades. Their two children played a new generation of games under the trees and in the attic. Eventually, Jane Harris, living by herself in the constantly needy house, opted for simpler accommodations and moved to New Hampshire. More than 350 years of history were bought by the people of Medfield to call their own.

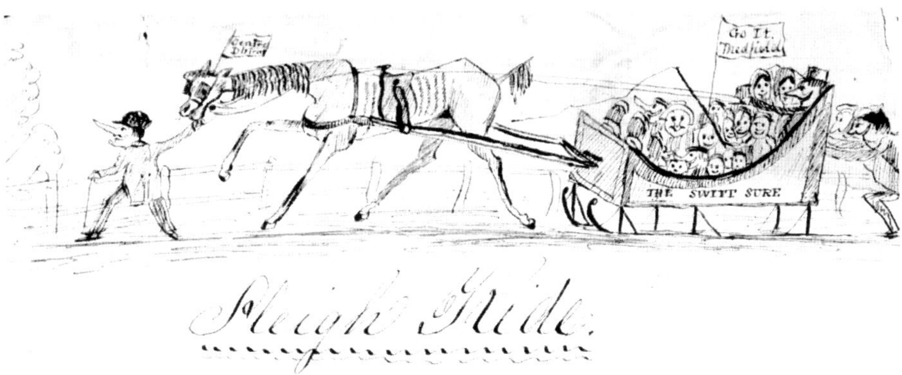

Sleigh Ride, 1839, drawing by George H. Derby. Another generation's idea of fun. Derby probably drew himself as the long-nosed character flanked by smiling females. "Go it Medfield," the banner says. *USMA Archives, George Derby Papers.*

CYCLES

Houses evolve in cycles of maintenance and disrepair. In New England, at least, the cycles recur every fifty years or so as the roof wears out, bricks lose their mortar, siding dries in the sun or rots in the damp, powder-post beetles or carpenter ants make inroads on the frame. Inside the aging house the plaster cracks, furnace fails, pipes rust out. Even the best-tended gardens need replanting. The house on Frairy Street had reached that point of no return by 1995, when Jane Harris decided to sell rather than try to cope with one more thing going wrong. The rest of the story is recent history, nowhere near as dramatic as the centuries of building past. A brief sketch, though, of the first five or six years of preservation work by the town suggests how much a labor of love saving an old house can be. It also suggests that persistence can get it done.

1995

- Late summer 1995, a grass-roots campaign begins when passersby see that the old Dwight-Derby House is vacant. The owner moves to New Hampshire and rumors circulate that developers want to tear the house down and build condos. By fall, windows are boarded up. The site exudes a sense of abandonment and decay. Richard DeSorgher, president of the Medfield Historical Society, begins holding weekly meetings with a group investigating options of what might be done to save the house.
- Winter 1995–96: The Medfield Historical Society establishes a formal study committee on the Dwight-Derby House, including members of the Board of Selectmen.

1996

- April: An article is placed on the annual town meeting warrant to see if the town would purchase the house. An agreement cannot be reached, however, with the owner, Mrs. Harris, prior to town meeting. The article is withdrawn.
- May: Town meeting gives overwhelming support to the Medfield Historical Society committee to (1) continue to pursue purchase of the house and (2) bring another article before the town if agreement can be reached with Mrs. Harris.
- The selectmen appoint an official town committee to explore ways to acquire and preserve the house; Mike Taylor, chairman.
- Summer: Mrs. Harris publicly lists the house for sale; initial asking price $350,000.
- September, Medfield Day: Mrs. Harris gives committee members permission to open the "as is" building to interested viewers; sheets hung from the second-story windows read SAVE THIS HOUSE.
- September: Architectural historians Tom Lingel and Rick Detwiller, as well as structural engineers inspecting the house, report that it is more of a historical treasure than was suspected; in fact, it is one of the oldest and most structurally undisturbed houses they have ever seen, especially on the interior.
- Fall: A purchase agreement is reached with Mrs. Harris; article is placed on the fall town meeting warrant, and in a near unanimous vote, the town approves $250,000 for purchase of the house plus $50,000 to stabilize it for the upcoming winter. Long-range planning envisions this property as a public education and meeting site with exhibition and special events space.

- Fall: "The Friends of the Dwight Derby House cordially invite you to a Wine and Cheese Pledge Night to officially kick off fundraising for the Derby House restoration. Zullo Gallery, Main Street, Medfield." The Zullo, Medfield's only art gallery, lends an air of respectability to this group of historical types aiming to fix up a decrepit old building.
- Dwight-Derby Committee is officially organized as a permanent subcommittee of the Medfield Historical Society representing the interests of the house; Richard DeSorgher elected chair. The earlier selectmen's committee is phased out.[137]

1997

- January: Friends of the Dwight-Derby House incorporate as a nonprofit organization. They receive certification from the Office of the Attorney General (Division of Public Charities) permitting them to solicit funds by mail—an obscure but essential regulation.
- The committee focuses on fundraising activities under the chairmanship of Geralyn Warren and Lisa Sharff. They set a goal of sponsoring at least one event per month to fund matching grants for the analysis and preservation activities needed before the property could be used extensively. Many events take place at the house, giving townspeople a chance to see the condition and potential of Medfield's newest old building. Events include:
  - chamber music concert by local Boston Symphony Orchestra musicians;
  - exhibition of nineteenth-century landscape artist J.S. Monks paintings;
  - display of Medfield Historical Society and privately owned quilts;
  - annual Garden Club spring plant sale;
  - house becomes starting point for Discover Medfield History Day trolley tour;
  - during slow event months, house is open for tours on one weekend day.

  Other fundraising efforts reach out to a broader public.
- A town-wide mailing of a Dwight-Derby newsletter keeps the fundraising effort up front in residents' minds, while informing them of progress made.
- The Medfield Historical Society devotes its monthly bulletins and meetings to the house and Dwight-Derby Committee efforts.
- Notecards with drawings of historic Medfield buildings by Westwood artist Jane Sugrue are sold in area stores, all proceeds going to the house fund.

- Donations in first months reach $65,000 in cash and kind. Donors are varied and creative: $5,000 from the Medfield Garden Club, $100 from each house sold by Medfield Properties Real Estate, $600 from Dale Street School grade two in their Chores to Restore program. Some of the fundraising urgency came from a National Trust for Historic Preservation grant deadline. The trust's Preservation Services Fund offered a one-to-one matching grant of $5,000, which would pay for professional evaluation of the house's historic development and its contemporary requirements. It was important for the committee to struggle for this one, because any possible funding for future work on the house was dependent on a comprehensive, down-to-earth analysis of what was there and what needed to be done. It seemed like magic when the match was raised and the grant was awarded.
- A Research and Planning Task Force is appointed, chaired by Electa Tritsch and Jackie Wile. The task force researches family and house history, explores potential usage, surveys public opinion on usage and conducts visits to comparable sites.
- August: *Historic Structures Report, Phase I* completed by Robert Major and Mary Turkel of the Preservation Cooperative, Ltd., with historical architect Lawrence Sorli. Report describes architectural evolution of house, assesses current conditions and recommends immediate necessary repairs.
- Friends committee decides to apply for $100,000 matching grant from the Massachusetts Historical Commission Preservation Projects Fund. The house must first be nominated to the National Register of Historic Places. Selectmen worry that the required Preservation Restriction might limit their options if the property does not prove to be financially independent, but eventually approve the grant application.
- October: Harvest Ball fundraiser at the American Legion hall.

<u>1998</u>

- April: Medfield Town Meeting votes to impose a permanent Preservation Restriction on the Dwight-Derby House property, limiting exterior alterations and protecting the building from demolition.
- Summer: Independent Archaeological Consulting (IAC) conducts Phase I site examination of areas to be impacted by construction activity.
- September: Harvest Fair with crafts, food and activities outside and inside the house.
- October 1998–May 1999: The Preservation Cooperative, Ltd., d/b/a Governor Street Restoration Contractors thoroughly stabilize, repair

and preserve the Dwight-Derby House exterior. The completion report reads: "Special mention should be given to the trio of carpenters who accomplished much of the heaviest—and most delicate—work: foreman Thomas D'Ovidio, William Bennett and Marc Medeiros. They are a great team."

1999

- April: Follow-up fieldwork is done by IAC to mitigate potential effects of foundation repair and regrading.
- Foundation repointed, bulkhead rebuilt, yard graded to drain away from foundation.
- House is painted by Paul Corey of Dedham, working from a paint analysis that uncovered colors from three different periods. The yellow color used was actually chosen by popular vote on Medfield Day, when cardboard sample houses were displayed in three historic color options: gray, white and yellow. Yellow synchronized with the most recent period of reconstruction, which the committee had independently decided to adhere to as much as possible.
- *Dwight Derby Cultural Landscape Report* prepared by Landscapes, a Vermont firm specializing in historic sites. Report includes site history, existing conditions, recommended treatment options and maintenance plan.

2000

- Fundraising focuses on Phase II of preservation work: the breezeway. In addition to special events, an annual appeal letter provides a solid source of funding. A $15,000 grant from a New York–based family foundation boosts the figures.
- The Preservation Cooperative, working with a structural engineer, prepares *Historic Structures Report, Phase II*, addressing the house interior, barn and breezeway.
- Mary Derby's music room revamped as the Medfield 350th Shoppe, selling gifts and memorabilia during the town's anniversary year.

2001

- February: Medfield second graders hold a "penny drive" that raises $850 for a flagpole to go on the Dwight-Derby House front lawn.
- March: Vintage clothing exhibit is cosponsored by the Friends and Medfield's 350th Anniversary Committee, with proceeds split between the two organizations. Joint sponsorship engages a wider range of people with the building and its other projects.

- September: Medfield's 350th Anniversary Ball is held in Meetinghouse Park. The spotlighted Dwight-Derby House serves as backdrop, reflected in the pond.

The story of the Dwight-Derby House is still unfolding. In 2002, the breezeway was rebuilt. Since then, the house has undergone interior paint analysis followed by repair, painting and reglazing in many rooms. That in turn led to the discovery of coarse brick "nogging"—an early colonial form of wall insulation—inside a single closet wall. The site has been opened to public receptions and private functions; offered second graders and high schoolers intimate glimpses of Medfield's past; and engaged descendants of Derbys and Dwights in exploring their family history. As recently as 2009, dendrochronology tests on the building frame revised previous construction-dating theories. Restoration carpenters are at work on the barn, once again stabilizing the structure that was judged to be beyond saving one hundred years ago. The men find hatch marks cut by earlier carpenters to match up beam ends. They hear the voices of history as they make history of their own.

The land on Frairy Street, the house built by Dwights and Derbys and the citizens of Medfield, is a piece of shared history. It is a product of determination, enthusiasm, stubbornness and vision, adapting to change and surviving its losses along the way. It stands today because of 350 years of love and persistence, a worthwhile example for us all.

Dwight-Derby House-Circa 1651

Open House--Art Display

Paintings by famed turn-of-the-century Medfield Artist J.A.S. Monks

Social 7--10 p.m.

hments 11a.m--2p.m
es / children welcomed)

oldest houses in America

greeters Thelma Spicer, right, and Jennifer O'Malley welcome Stephen and Corinne Donovan to the town-owned Dwight Derby House Saturday morning.

A modern-day barn-raising

Town comes together for fund-raiser

bel

DFIELD – For the roup of volunteers that as organized to support e oldest house in Med-

"We're very excited. The feedback from the townspeople, I think, has

"We're very excited," said De Sorgher, chairman of the of the Dwight-Derby House "The feedback from the tow ple, I think, has been incred The group held a fund-ra rday, complete with a f band and hosts decke ial garb. After walking airy Street house, on said it was like being ridge Village. ugh the house looks r outside, those who c

, PAGE 2B

GLOBE PHOTO / DENNIS VANDAL

DeSorgher, chairman of the Friends of the Dwight-Derby House, surveys the site of the 346-year-ield landmark, which the group is hoping to rehabilitate for use as a community center.

De
go
fo

By LAURA

Applaus selectmen enabling

PAGE 8, December 12, 1996, Medfield Suburban Press

Structural engineer fills in

Dwight-Derby House given clean bill of health just in

11/21/96

Historic house agreement proves troubling

To the Editor:

We were shocked to read in the Nov. 7 Medfield Suburban Press that the Board of Selectmen negotiated an agreement with some members of the Friends of the Dwight-Derby House agreeing to a Feb. 15, 1997, deadline for the raising of $100,000. Failure to meet that deadline allows the

Letters

motion itself likely would have changed, given this information. Second, the spirit of the debate at Town Meeting was overwhelmingly in support of giving the ad hoc committee a reasonable opportunity to raise funds

Meeting raise serious questions whether the selectmen are acting in a legal and politic manner.

It seems appropriate that the selectmen cease and desist from any further action relating to the Dwight-Derby House and allow regular Town Meeting the opportunity to decide, incorporating all relevant information, as to what constitutes a reason-

TIN 1997 (VOL 34 NO 1) THE MEDFIELD HISTORICAL SOCIETY ANNOUNCES 7 EVE

Dwight Derby H

MER, 1885

...graph was taken before 1885
...berlsin Photography Studios,
...ard, Maine & Medfield, Mass.
It shows
...studio, with sign,
...home, with porch,
...the John Dwight house
...ed in the Meetinghouse Pond
...a summer's day
...e than 110 years ago.

...rticle to purchas...
...erby House
...ins easy passage

10/31

...AN DAVIS
...dents voted overwhelmingly
... night to purchase the
...Derby House on Frairy
...or $225,000 under the stipu-
...the Historical Society raise
...o restore the 345-year-old

•Schools net $160,000, page 14
•Civil Defense gets ne... home, page 15
•How articles fared, p... 15

1997

Dwight-Derby House

"Fall Harvest Ball"

• Dwight-Derby News •

Volume 2, Issue 2

Spring, 1999

WE DID IT!

Underneath It All

Exterior preservation of the Dwight-Derby House has been accomplished thanks to a grant from the Massachusetts Preservation Projects Fund, and the work of a dozen highly skilled artisans.

Beginning with an archeological survey done during the dog days of last August, the House and its immediate surroundings have been thoroughly examined, tested, and then structurally preserved.

A four-person field crew from Independent ...

...group gets
...ad to apply
...e grant

...y night as
...y papers
...tomorrow's

'They've be...
supportive...

Derby House group pushes ahead with fund-raisers

By SUSAN O'KEEFE

Structural engineer to visit site today

With more than $30,000 in pledges since fund-raising began in September, the Friends of the Dwight-Derby House are well on their way toward raising $100,0...

...bers of the Boston Symphony Orchestra is planned for January. But before visitors can ...

...neer and the nod from the Board of Selectmen.

A structural engineer is check-...

...sound, the committee can go ahead with their plans for the fund-raisers.

"There is liability [if someone gets hurt], but there would be liability on any town property," said Town Counsel Mark Cerel.

...the house last week and jumped on the floor in one of the rooms to test its soundness.

"There was china everywhere and when I jumped, none of the china shook," Gagliani said, trying to explain how sturdy the ...

...ng pieces
...open house Saturday

Notes

Chapter 1

1. Dwight roots in England were ferreted out of original parish records by Victor Peskett of Metfield (Norfolk), England. His patience and skill at deciphering seventeenth-century penmanship, as well as his lifelong scholarship in East Anglian history and genealogy, made the beginning of this story possible.
2. A conjectural reconstruction based on other Dwight wills.
3. There are no ship's records documenting the Dwights' transatlantic passage. The date of their sailing is inferred from two scraps of information. First, Mary Dwight's birth was recorded in the Dedham vital records as having taken place on July 25, 1635 (before the town was founded). Many years later Mary, by then wife of Henry Phillips, died; her funeral was attended by inveterate journalist Samuel Sewall, who commented that Mrs. Phillips had been born at sea—thus plausibly dating the Dwight family's immigration to 1635. Robert Hanson, personal communication, 1997.
4. Don Gleason Hill, ed., *Dedham Records* (Dedham, MA: Dedham Transcript, 1888), 3:47.
5. *Dedham Records*, 2:14.
6. *Dedham Records*, 2:24.
7. Karen Dacey, *In the Shadow of the Great Blue Hill* (Lanham, MD: University Press of America, 1995) documents Eliot's Indian village efforts.
8. Despite that, the first mill was not constructed until forty years later, when Thomas Sawin built a gristmill on a tributary brook of the Charles. See

Electa Tritsch, *Men of Useful Trades* (Westwood, MA: Dedham Grant Survey Project, 1981).

9. *Dedham Records*, 3:130. An extensive series of government and court papers concerning this controversy, which went on for years, is published verbatim in Frank Smith's *History of Dover, Massachusetts* (Dover, MA: Dover Historical Society, 1897).

10. A series of European disease epidemics in 1616–17 killed up to 90 percent of the Native American population living within twenty or thirty miles of the Atlantic coast. In 1633, smallpox eradicated most of the remaining native inhabitants. See Barbara E. Luedtke, *The Camp at the Bend in the River* (Boston: Massachusetts Historical Commission, 1985), 311.

11. *Dedham Records*, 3:181.

12. William S. Tilden, *History of the Town of Medfield, Massachusetts* (Boston: Geo. H. Ellis, 1887). Tilden, our only source, lists between four and seven selectmen for any one year.

13. Not actually surprising, since in those first years of settlement little fencing had been built and much of the livestock roamed free. When a cow wandered into someone else's home field or a sheep strayed too far from the flock, they were relegated to the pound to be collected by their owners.

14. Timothy Dwight estate inventory taken March 6 and entered March 15, 1676/77. Suffolk County Registry of Probate, Boston, MA, 12:131. Acreage is approximate due to one entry listed simply as "a parcel of land."

15. Information about farming in this and the following paragraphs owes much to a journal kept over a twenty-year period by David Choate of Essex, Massachusetts, now in the Essex Historical Society. Although Choate was farming in Essex County a century after Timothy Dwight, the rhythms and frustrations of the agricultural year had not changed substantially.

16. Crops are all listed in Dwight's 1677 inventory. The inclusion of wheat is surprising, since a wheat blight effectively wiped out that crop in Massachusetts during the 1660s. It does appear on a number of early Medfield lists, however, in payment of taxes and the town's subscription to Harvard College (see Tilden, *History*).

17. For example, in Hingham at one of the town's first planting fields, called World's End, the natural causeway that connected two peninsulas was a regular issue in town affairs. One seventeenth-century vote specifically decided to raise the causeway above high tide

level, indicating that it had previously been allowed to flood twice a day. *Town Records of Hingham, Massachusetts, 163*. Microfilm at Hingham Public Library.

18. Twentieth-century information from Ken Feeney and Bobbie Kennedy Sr. of the Medfield Public Works Dept., personal communication, 1998.
19. Philip J. Greven Jr., *Four Generations* (Ithaca, NY, and London: Cornell University Press, 1970), is a classic study of the impact and limitations of partible inheritance.
20. Best known among his descendants was Timothy IV (1752–1817), president of Yale College.
21. Quoted in Tilden, *History*, 72; from Mass. Archives 67:52. Petition received May 11, agreed May 21, 1668.
22. Francis S. Drake, *The Town of Roxbury…* (Boston: Municipal Printing Office, 1905), 370.
23. John Frairy estate inventory, 1675. Suffolk Probate, miscellaneous docket, vol. 8.
24. including Frederick Detwiller and Abbott Lowell Cummings
25. Dendrochronological testing completed in 2009, too late to revise this chapter, seems to point to this addition being built about 1696 by John Dwight, rather than by his father (John Thompson, personal communication). If this revision is correct, the reader will have to "revise" his imagination of this scene, as well.
26. Corn and wheat were perfectly marketable commodities, but in this case, Harvard College was the loser. A letter from the minister and selectmen to the college, written after many of Medfield's barns were burned the following February, requests that for those whose property was destroyed, "the fourteen bushells of Indian Corne, and one bushell of wheat then subscribed we humbly desire those p'sons may be excused" (quoted in Tilden, *History*, 94).
27. A remarkably small number, considering the seventy to eighty families—a conservative three hundred residents—who lived in the town, and that as many as half the houses were reputed to have been destroyed.
28. Timothy Dwight will, written March 3, 1765/66; entered March 15, 1676/77. Suffolk Probate 6:179.
29. Timothy Jr. appears to have been ill or otherwise debilitated. The dying father comments in his will, "if my son Timothy live and grow up to [marry]"—implying that there was serious doubt that he would do so. (SP 6:179)
30. Ibid.

31. No seventeenth-century barns are known to be standing in eastern New England, but a useful source for comparative information is P.S. Barnwell, Colum Giles and A.T. Adams, *English Farmsteads, 1750–1914* (Swindon, England: Royal Commission on the Historical Monuments of England, 1997).
32. Dwight inventory; Suffolk Probate 12:131. "Fairly" safe was a conclusion reached in 1996, when some attic floorboards were removed to inspect ceiling beams. A sizable cache of corncobs and acorns attested to the attic's occupation by squirrels or mice on more than one occasion.
33. Peter Adams's will, entered 1690. Suffolk Probate New Series 3:186.
34. Despite the in-town connection, John and Elizabeth married in Dedham because the new minister chosen by the Medfield church—the Reverend Joseph Baxter—was even younger than John Dwight, and was not ordained until 1697.
35. Judge Samuel Sewall, writing in 1697 and quoted in Tilden, *History*, 107.
36. Later alterations have obliterated any above-ground evidence of this room, but the lack of cellar in this corner of the house supports the idea that a cool room was once present. This milk room or buttery was commonly found in colonial farmhouses. A later (1784) local example is seen in the Caryl House in Dover, Massachusetts, a town-owned property managed by the Dover Historical Society.
37. Tilden describes the Fisher land as being in "what is now Dover, on the lower side of the corners near Farm Bridge" (389). The division of property between John and Seth Dwight in 1740 included forty-seven acres bounded north on the Natick line and south on the Medfield line—in other words, the same vicinity. Suffolk Deeds 60:273.
38. See section "Star Crossed" for further discussion of intrafamilial land transfers between Horatio Townsend and Mary Townsend Derby. It is likely that this property was considered Seth Dwight's inheritance and valued accordingly, so the purchase price would be factored into his inheritance after John Dwight's death.
39. John Dwight to Seth Dwight, deed written November 25, 1740; recorded September 2, 1741. Suffolk Deeds 60:273.

CHAPTER 2

40. Townsend Family Book, Dedham Historical Society.
41. John Dwight's probate inventory, written six years later, includes "Joynery & Carpenter's Tools" (Suffolk Probate 45:107).

42. The "mansion house" reference is from an 1836 deed transferring title to Anstis Townsend (Norfolk Deeds 112:13). In England, the term "manse" was specifically applied to a minister's house, but it is not clear that the practice carried over to the colonies. The house itself, according to Tilden, burned down in 1876 when it was being used as part of D.D. Curtis & Co.'s straw hat factory. A lithograph on page 263 of Tilden's *History* (bottom image) may represent the original Townsend house.
43. Townsend Family Book, Dedham Historical Society.
44. Tilden, *History*, 374.
45. Ibid., 438.
46. Hannah Dwight's will, written March 2, 1786; entered August 2, 1792. Suffolk Probate 91:523.
47. How Spring came to be involved in this situation is pure speculation. He may have known Timothy Dwight, a fellow doctor, or may have been acquainted with Dr. James Gerauld, a Medfield physician who served as selectman with Jonathan Metcalf. In any case, it appears that Spring bought the property primarily as an investment, allowing widow Hannah Dwight to remain in the house until her death in 1792.
48. Administration of Moses Hill's estate, first administrator's account, June 4, 1799. Norfolk Probate #9483.
49. George H. was the first of eight Derbys and related family members to attend the academy.
50. Lorenzo Sabine, *Biographical Sketches of Loyalists of the American Revolution* (Boston: Little, Brown and Company, 1864), 2:361.
51. Property confiscation, somewhat like modern foreclosure, was often more a paper transaction than a literal removal of goods. In the case of Gregory's Medfield house, brother Samuel was allowed to purchase the property, and he almost immediately turned it over to the Reverend Jonathan's family.
52. Sabine, *Sketches*, identifies a number of Massachusetts and Connecticut Hubbards who were Episcopalian and Loyalist in their sympathies, including at least a half dozen who went to Nova Scotia. Whether this branch of the family was equally Loyalist or whether, like the Townsends, their allegiance was mixed is not known.
53. Sarah Townsend to Gregory Townsend, September 1, 1782. Townsend Family Papers 1676–1877, Massachusetts Historical Society. (Hereafter cited as Townsend Papers MHS)
54. Thomas Greene to Nathaniel Greene, October 1790. Townsend Papers MHS.

55. Sarah Townsend to Mary Hubbard, January 18, 1797. Townsend Papers MHS.
56. Administration of Hill estate (NP #9483) also deed, Hill estate to Horatio Townsend, December 3, 1798 (Norfolk Deeds 10:33).
57. Sarah Townsend to Mary Hubbard, February 25, 1805. Townsend Papers MHS.
58. www.en.wikipedia.org/wiki/Hannah_Adams.
59. *Dedham Gazette*, January 22, 1870, and August 10, 1867.
60. John Derby's receipt for payment, August 1816. Derby Family Papers, Phillips Library, Peabody Essex Museum, Salem, MA. (Hereafter cited as Derby Family Papers PEM)
61. Mary Townsend Derby to Sarah Townsend, March 9, 1821. Townsend Papers MHS.

Chapter 3

62. Mary Townsend and John Barton Derby to Horatio Townsend Jr., July 22, 1819. George H. Derby Papers, Box 2, Special Collections & Archives Division, United States Military Academy Library, West Point, NY. (Hereafter cited as Derby Papers USMA)
63. Horatio Jr. eventually became a physician, serving as a naval ship's doctor during the 1830s and '40s, his voyages apparently focused on South America. In 1840, he shipped home the pocket watch he had inherited from Great-Uncle Gregory, to be given to George Derby. In 1846, he trained in the new craft of photography and wrote that he was planning to return to Valparaiso to pursue this new career. According to a family genealogy, he died in South America sometime after 1846. Townsend Papers MHS.
64. Mary Townsend to Sarah Townsend, February 1820. Townsend Papers MHS.
65. Draft letter written by Horatio Townsend to John Derby's father. Derby Papers USMA, Box 2.
66. Townsend Family Book, Dedham Historical Society.
67. Nathaniel Greene to Mary Townsend, July 12, 1820. Derby Papers USMA, Box 2.
68. Mary Derby to Sarah Townsend, December 27, 1820. Townsend Papers MHS.
69. Ibid, January 9, 1821.
70. Horatio Townsend bond written May 14, 1821; entered March 3, 1823. Norfolk Deeds 65:90.

71. Anstis Townsend to Mary Derby, June 13, 1821. Townsend Papers MHS.
72. Mary Derby to Sarah Townsend, June 17, 1821. Derby Papers USMA.
73. Mary Derby to Sarah Townsend, February 7, 1822. Townsend Papers MHS.
74. Ibid.
75. John Barton Derby to Anstis Townsend, May 23, 1822. Townsend Papers MHS.
76. Mary Derby to Sarah Townsend, March 4, 1825. Townsend Papers MHS.
77. Medfield Vital Records.
78. *Dedham Records*, 2:219.
79. Deed, John Barton Derby to Elias Hasket Derby, December 1822 (Norfolk Deeds 71:107), and deed, Horatio Townsend to Mary Derby, dated October 1, 1823, entered August 3, 1829 (Norfolk Deeds 88:31).
80. Deeds, John Derby to Elias Derby, Norfolk Deeds 76:52 and 77:194. Both written February 13, 1823, recorded 1825. The leased acres were part of the "ministerial land" given to the Congregational church after John Frairy's death in 1675. The land was still providing annual income by being leased to local farmers, who used it for hayfields.
81. Townsend to Derby. Norfolk Deeds 88:31.
82. Mary Derby to Sarah Townsend, June 30, 1823, and Lucretia Townsend to Sarah Townsend, October 31, 1823. Townsend Papers MHS.
83. Julia Butterfield may have been wife of Pitts Butterfield, a Dedham leather dresser who died in 1822.
84. Mary Derby to Sarah Townsend, March 27, 1825. Townsend Papers MHS.
85. Thirty-five years later, the 1860 federal census listed women's occupations for the first time. Ironically, long after Mary had stopped needing employment, she chose to list her occupation as "Bonnet maker." It is hard not to think of this as a declaration of support for honest women's work.
86. Mary Derby to Sarah Townsend, July 10, 1826. Townsend Papers MHS.
87. Lucretia Townsend to Mary Derby, May 6, 1827. Derby Papers USMA.
88. *Dedham Gazette*, August 10, 1867. This was actually part of an obituary for John Barton Derby, but the writer found nearly as much to say about the son as the father.
89. "George H. Derby Humorist and Satirist." Paper presented to Medfield Historical Society, 1896; typescript in Medfield Historical Society.

90. Derby Papers USMA. The West Point collection of Derby's drawings include a number of his Medfield home, from a cartoon sketch showing mother and aunt at the upper windows to a more sophisticated landscape drawn from a perspective across Meetinghouse Pond.
91. Lucretia Townsend to George Derby, January 19, 1838. Derby Papers USMA, Box 7.
92. *Dedham Gazette*, August 10, 1867.
93. Nomination letter by William S. Hastings, February 26, 1842. Derby Papers USMA. Mary was never legally divorced from John Barton Derby.
94. Cover letter by Mary Derby, July 19, 1841. Derby Papers USMA.
95. Especially notable are John C. Waugh's *The Class of 1846* (New York: Random House, 1994) and George R. Stewart's *John Phoenix, Esq.: The Veritable Squibob* (New York: Henry Holt & Co., 1937). Interestingly, Stewart based much of his work on materials that in the 1930s were still in Derby family hands. These were the same materials later deposited by family members in the USMA Archives, providing an invaluable resource for the present book.
96. L. Quigley to Mary Derby, August 12, 1859. Derby Papers USMA, Box 8.
97. W.A. Wells (Andover Teachers' Seminary) to Mary Derby, January 26, 1838. Derby Papers USMA, Box 7.
98. This was one of the designations in John and Hasket Derby's deeds. Another called it "the Bottom road," while Sarah Townsend's will refers to pastureland "on the Frary road so called."
99. Will of Sarah (Aunt Sally) Townsend, written 1830; entered 1836. Norfolk Probate #18680.
100. *Dedham Gazette*, "John Barton Derby," January 22, 1870.
101. J.B. Derby, "A Vision," Boston, 1848. Copy at PEM Phillips Library. This description bears significant resemblance to descriptions of George Horatio Derby's last illness.
102. J.B. Derby, "Musings of a Recluse," Boston, 1837. Copy at PEM Phillips Library.
103. Ibid., 80.
104. J.B. Derby, "Woman," Boston, 1839, 8, "On the Birth of a Daughter." Copy at PEM Phillips Library.
105. *Dedham Records*, 2: 219.
106. *Dedham Gazette*, August 10, 1867.
107. Aunt Lucretia Townsend Greene of Boston, Anstis's sister-in-law. Her will was written 1842. Derby Papers USMA, Box 11.

108. Mary Derby to Theron Metcalf, May 3, 1842. Townsend Papers MHS. Metcalf replied that an 1834 Massachusetts legislative ruling confirmed the legality of all pre-1834 marriages, despite their having been performed by a justice or minister who may have been functioning outside his normal authority or jurisdiction. This law was undoubtedly passed in response to the clerical disruption caused by the "New Light"/"Old Light" schism that had transpired in the Congregational Church during the late teens and twenties. It was Mary Derby's misfortune to be shackled by a ruling intended to free couples from dubious marriage contracts.

109. Evidence of a persistent wet basement was dug up by preservation carpenters repairing the cellar stairs in 1998. Buried under later fill was a slate-lined trench running from the back to the front of the house, evidently intended to channel an unstoppable subterranean stream through the building and into the pond beyond. The effort was unsuccessful. In 1998, repairs had to be postponed until the surrounding water table went down in dry summer weather.

110. The two attic rooms are not well understood. One, at the east end, was never finished and was used as a playroom for later inhabitants of the house. It is interesting for its exposed construction details, including a door frame recycled as part of the nineteenth-century dormer window framing, and the wooden shingles that still remain on an earlier roof section protected by the dormer gable. The west room, clearly used as a bedchamber, has an unusual barrel-vaulted ceiling, finished knee walls and evidence that it once had a small stove. The dating of these details is not known.

111. A spectacular fire that destroyed the Baker & Cushman carriage factory in 1868 may have been the impetus for slate roofing. Scorch marks inside the west end of the attic suggest that sparks from the blaze may have damaged the old wooden-shingled roof.

112. Untitled poem signed "Geo H Derby," dated June 13, 1852. Derby Papers USMA, Box 8.

113. USMA cemetery records, included with Derby Papers USMA.

114. A comment included in John B. Derby's obituary, *Dedham Gazette*, August 10, 1867.

115. Federal census, population, 1880. Medfield: Roll 547, ED 499 as of June 1, 1880.

116. Will of Mary Derby, written 1879, entered October 13, 1880. Norfolk Probate #22092.

117. Mentioned in George Derby's 1852 poem.

118. *Norfolk County Gazette*, September 18, 1880. Microfilm at the Dedham Historical Society. *Cholera morbus* was an old term for acute gastroenteritis.

CHAPTER 4

119. The Never-Ending Dig finally ended because it became too unwieldy to coordinate. The project involved busing every seventh-grade class to a privately owned property where students would learn topography, study flora and fauna and spend an exciting hour digging, sifting and recording finds from an early twentieth-century coal ash and trash pile. The project was never without its critics, especially among professional archaeologists who disapproved of nonprofessional excavation. To its credit, the dig and its tireless coordinators succeeded in educating a whole student generation on the value and fragility of archaeological sites.

120. The same was true of the three centuries of privies that must have been associated with the house. Wells and privies, filled in and sealed after use, are archaeological treasures containing a time capsule of trash and garbage that can be used to address a wide range of questions concerning human behavior. To date, still no sign of privies has been found at the Dwight-Derby House. Speculative placement of one adjacent to the carriage house is based on a single bird's-eye view of the property and on common nineteenth-century practice.

121. Comprehensive reports on the firm's two-year excavations were prepared for the Friends of the Dwight-Derby House, with copies filed at the Massachusetts Historical Commission. Kathleen Wheeler and Ellen Marlatt, "Findings from the 1998 Site Examination at the Dwight Derby House, Medfield Massachusetts," February 8, 1999, and Kathleen Wheeler, "Findings from the 1999 Site Examination and Data Recovery, Dwight-Derby House, Medfield," October 20, 2000.

122. Note apparently from Lucretia to Sarah, who was in Boston, January 16, 1825. Townsend Papers MHS. There was much speculation as to why a thimble, a prized possession, should have ended up deposited in the dirt. Restoration carpenters theorized that the thimble had been lost in a gap that was plainly visible between parlor floorboard and baseboard, where it rested on the house sill until it eventually rolled outside the building when the sill rotted, twisting outward under the weight of the wall it was meant to support.

123. A report on excavations and findings is on file at the Massachusetts Historical Commission. John Thompson and Electa Kane Tritsch, "Report on Emergency Data Recovery, Dwight-Derby House Breezeway…May–June 2002," April 2009.
124. This and subsequent Battelle excerpts from Derby Papers USMA, Box 10.
125. An undated newspaper clipping in the Medfield Historical Society notes that "Lieutenant Colonel Derby and wife have been recent visitors here. [He] is stationed at St. Paul, Minnesota." That and an earlier calling card (he was then titled "Major") attest to at least two visits to the family homestead.
126. Richard P. DeSorgher, *History of the Town of Medfield, Massachusetts 1887–1925* (Medfield Historical Society, 1999), 59, 68, 80; Baker & Cushman photo (circa 1910), 345.
127. Census records from the early 1900s do not give addresses for residents, while contemporary maps and tax lists name owners only ("M.T. Derby heirs").
128. From undated newspaper clippings in Medfield Historical Society files.
129. See discussion throughout DeSorgher, *History*, of complaints about tramps and incidents of ethnic prejudice in the period 1887–1925.
130. Letter and advertisement donated to Friends of the Dwight-Derby House by Virginia Derby Jordan, 2009.
131. The color, approximating that of the Longfellow House in Cambridge, may actually have been popularized by Sears and Roebuck's prefab building division in the early twentieth century, as Sears's top-of-the-line offering was a smaller version of that building. (Longfellow House docent personal communication, 2009)
132. Margaret Black registered the property in Land Court in March 1943 [LC Cert. 29083]; it was bought by Louisa Hackett of Dedham in December 1945 [LC Cert 32243], who sold it to Theodore C. Baker of Belmont, "husband of Mary Amory Baker," in June 1948 [LC Cert 37015]. Edith Clifford Prescott Baker was his mother.
133. Augusta Thorndike to Caroline and Mike Standley, January 16, 1997. Private collection.
134. Knowledge and interpretation of colonial New England house interiors has undergone a revolution since then. Interested readers are referred to recent research and publications by Historic New England, Inc., as well as the Colonial Williamsburg Foundation.

135. Thorndike to Standley, 1997.

136. Bob Thorndike, personal communication, 1996.

137. Subsequent chairs of what became the Friends Committee include Mike Standley, Monica Bushnell, Tim Sullivan and John Thompson.

Index

E

F

G

H

I

R

S

T

U

V

W

About the Author

W. Gelbart photo.

Electa Kane Tritsch's long history career has run the gamut from teacher to archaeologist, community organizer to historical society guru, as she has written about the men and women who built, treasured and preserved Massachusetts.

A longtime resident of Medfield, where she helped save the Dwight-Derby House, she moved to Concord in 2004 and directs her own research firm. Other regional books by this author include *Building Dedham* and *Old Wives Tales.*